A Sac

*Marie Adèle Garnier and the
founding of Tyburn Convent*

By
DOM BEDE CAMM

Saint Michael's Abbey Press
Saint Michael's Abbey
Farnborough
Hampshire GU14 7NQ

Telephone +44 (0) 1252 546 105
Facsimile +44 (0) 1252 372 822

www.farnboroughabbey.org
prior@farnboroughabbey.org

www.theabbeyshop.com

Original Edition:
The Foundress of Tyburn Convent,
Mother Mary of St Peter
Adèle Garnier (1934)

New Edition: Saint Michael's Abbey Press, 2006

ISBN 0 907077 45 5

A catalogue record for this book is available from the British Library.

Printed and bound by Newton Printing Ltd., London.

In obedience to the decrees of Pope Urban VIII and other Sovereign Pontiffs, the writer declares that the graces and other supernatural facts related in this volume as witnessing to the sanctity of Servants of God other than those canonized or beatified by the Church, rest on human authority alone; and in regard thereto, as in all things else, the writer submits himself without reserve to the infallible judgement of the Apostolic See, which alone has power and authority to pronounce as to whom rightly belong the Character and Title of Saint or Blessed.

DOM BEDE CAMM, OSB, MA, FSA.
February 21, 1934.

Contents

Introduction to the New Edition

'A SACRIFICE of Praise' is the fruit of the friendship that exists between the Benedictine monks of Farnborough and the nuns of Tyburn Convent. Its purpose is to furnish with information the many pilgrims who knock at Tyburn's door, and to update and perpetuate the work and memory of that revered friend of Tyburn, Dom Bede Camm, who first published this work under the title 'The Foundress of Tyburn Convent'.

Born in 1864 and educated at Westminster School and Keble College, Oxford, Camm became a Catholic in 1890, and a year later a Benedictine monk at the Belgian Abbey of Maredsous. The famed monastic observance and splendid liturgy there must have quickly proved home to one previously immersed in the ritualist movement of the Church of England. From 1896–1912 he served at Erdington Abbey in Birmingham, and shifted his Benedictine affiliation to the Abbey of Downside in 1913.

In 1902, Dom Bede heard the news that Mother Adèle Garnier and her community had purchased a house at Tyburn. These nuns, who had lived and prayed at Montmartre in Paris where St Denis and his companions had won the martyr's crown, now found themselves driven by Providence, and the political vicissitudes of France, to a place consecrated by the blood of the Martyrs of England.

News of their arrival brought great joy to English Catholics who loved and venerated the memory of their Martyrs. Dom Bede wrote to congratulate the nuns while they were still at Bassett Road, and Mother Adèle Garnier's reply marked the beginning of a friendship which lasted till her death, and indeed beyond. Thereafter, Dom Bede devoted himself to the Tyburn nuns and the shrine of the English Martyrs. He gathered relics, and helped adorn the crypt with various treasures: the magnificent Maredsous altar and reredos, the Carthusian painting, and the particularly lovely Margaret Roper windows in which the lives of the Martyrs are depicted in the Beatitudes and the Corporal Works of Mercy.

When poverty threatened the existence of the Tyburn community, Camm appealed to a generous public on their behalf, and left the copyrights to his writings to the nuns so that his practical support might continue even beyond his death. Other Tyburn friendships owed their genesis to him. Blessed Columba Marmion, served as spiritual director to the Foundress and did much to strengthen their Benedictine charism. Both Abbot Marmion and Bede Camm were also friends of, and regular visitors to, the monks of Farnborough.

Dom Bede's biography of the Foundress of Tyburn Convent reveals a high esteem for the person of Adèle Garnier and remains a permanent testimony to his reverence for, and devotion to, this great servant of God.

Dom Cuthbert Brogan OSB
Prior of Farnborough

chapter one

Childhood And Youth

THE subject of this memoir, Marie Adèle Garnier, was born on the Feast of the Assumption, August 15, 1838, and baptised on September 12, Feast of the Holy Name of Mary. Her parents were Nicholas Garnier, an architect and contractor, and his wife Denise, whose maiden name was Caiset. She was born at the little town of Grancey-le-Château, situated on the vine-clad hills of the Côte-d'Or in Burgundy. Grancey is, as its name implies, renowned chiefly for its ancient castle, of which the fourteenth-century chapel (once collegiate) boasts of many beautiful works of art. Here St Bernard finally found his vocation to the austere Cistercian life, while his brothers, who sought to keep him in the world, were engaged on the siege of the castle, under the leadership of Hugh Duke of Burgundy.

Marie Adèle Garnier, then, was a native of Burgundy, as were St Jane de Chantal and St Sophie Barat, foundress of the Sisters of the Sacred Heart. Burgundians are renowned in France for their good sense and sure judgement, and for their courtesy, gaiety and kindness of heart. All these characteristics, as we shall see, were possessed in a high degree by this child of predestination. She knew how to delight and charm those who surrounded her by her ready wit and clever repartees. There was never anything rigid or gloomy about her, but above all, as the late Cardinal Mercier remarked: 'Her simple presence was an invitation to come nearer to God.'

Her father, who was devoted to his children, was unfortunately not a practising Catholic, though always respectful and reverent towards religion; but her mother was a most fervent and devoted Christian. Of their marriage were born six children, first a little boy who died in infancy, then four girls, Louise, Joséphine, Marie and Adèle, and lastly a boy, Thomas, who was commonly known as Victor. Three years after Adèle's birth the family migrated from Grancey to the neighbouring town of Is–sur–Tille. This is a much larger place, situated on the right bank of the Ignon.

When Adèle was only six years old she had the misfortune to lose her mother. Before she died, Madame Garnier begged her husband to send her children to a convent that they might be prepared for their first Communion.

Shortly after Adèle's first Communion, M. Garnier, who had removed to Dijon, and was anxious to have his children nearer to him, took them away from Villeneuve, and placed them in one of the best schools in that city, the Pension Baillot. Adèle was then twelve years old. Three years later she, with her three elder sisters, settled down at home with their father, and for several years Adèle received her instruction from teachers who came to the house. The four sisters were devoted to one another; their gaiety and simplicity made them welcome at the houses of their many friends, who were charmed with their quick understanding and gentle ways. Victor was then studying at the University in preparation for his future career. Unfortunately he gradually ceased to practise his religion, although without ever losing his faith in God.

It may surprise us to find that Adèle, at the early age of sixteen, was betrothed to a young man of their acquaintance. It was not her own wish, but was, as was usual in France at the time, an affair arranged by her family. As she was so young, the engagement lasted for some years. As time wore on Adèle conceived a growing dislike for marriage, and more especially in this case as she knew that her fiancé was far from sharing her religious convictions. It is true that the young man had promised to allow to his future wife complete liberty in carrying out her religious duties and exercises of piety, but as a matter of fact his promises were of little value. This was clearly proved one day when Adèle, who was coming down the staircase, heard a conversation going on below between her fiancé and one of his friends. This young man was speaking of her, of her well-known piety, her devotion to her religion. The fiancé began to laugh. 'Oh! once married, I'll soon put an end to all that!' said he. Adèle at once ran down the stairs, and said to him: 'Sir, you will not have to take this trouble, for I shall never be your wife.' Nothing could change her decision, to the great despair of the young man. He even tried to commit suicide in her presence by thrusting into his breast a pair of scissors which one of the girls had left on the table.

M. Garnier lived only for his children. He always refused to think of a second marriage, and devoted himself to his profession and to his house. Joséphine and Adèle, who had a great talent for draughtmanship, used to help him in drawing his plans. (He was engaged on important constructions at Dijon.) Adèle was his child of predilection. In return his children loved and reverenced him with real devotion. In fact, it would be difficult to have found a more united and devoted family. Victor, who was to have a brilliant career as a naval engineer, proved himself an admirable brother and son. It was his joy, as time went on, to be able to contribute largely to the family expenses, and thus to augment their comfort.

Meanwhile Adèle began to feel drawn to a more perfect life, but not yet it would seem to holy religion. 'I began,' she writes, 'to despise the vanities of the world, to grieve over, perhaps rather to be ashamed of, my faults and defects, and I think that by God's grace I now began to correct them. My soul was constantly dwelling upon God and was filled with the longing to please Him. Little by little the desire for a life more laborious, more occupied, and at the same time more dependent on others, took hold of me, and I felt thus alone could I please my God. I asked my father if he would permit me to try to become a governess in a family. He gave his consent, and circumstances soon permitted me to find what I desired in an excellent family in the west of France.'

A family residing near Nantes asked her to become their governess. She, however, felt real repugnance to the idea. But Father Marquet told her authoritatively that she must accept the offer, and at the same time exhorted her to be faithful to her daily Communion. The de Crochard family with whom Adèle was destined to pass three years, happy years, filled with divine graces, was then living in the country not far from Angers. Their house, called Le Chatelet, is situated close to the village of Milon, and is therefore often known as the Château de Milon.

As time went on Adèle felt herself drawn more and more strongly to the devotion to the Sacred Heart of Jesus, and at the same time to the religious life. Her director recognised that she had a true vocation, but doubted if the weak state of her health would allow her to persevere. However, he consented to her making the trial, and at the age of twenty-six she entered the novitiate of the Society of the Sacred Heart at Conflans. But after she had spent two months there as a postulant her weak health necessitated her leaving the convent. She was almost in despair. She said herself she thought she would have died of grief, had not the sight of a great Crucifix turned her thoughts from herself and her sufferings to Jesus and His Passion. But her grief was so keen that she remained seriously ill for a whole year, and her only consolation was an invincible hope that Our Lord had not abandoned her.

She spent some time at Poitiers with the de Crochard family, and then went as governess to a Madame St Cyr, who was their friend. But her weak state of health would not allow her to remain there long, and she had to return to her family at Dijon to seek the repose she so greatly needed.

And here Our Lord favoured her with new graces. Sometimes at church she felt herself suddenly raised up to God by a supernatural force which filled her with unspeakable bliss. This did not last long, a minute, perhaps, but happened very frequently. She feared in her humility that this might be a delusion, due to her pride, and yet she could not bear to speak of it in confession. Her confessor, seeing her embarrassment, questioned her, and assured her that there was no sin, no pride in this; it was a very great grace granted her by God, for which she must thank Him in all humility. It was a sign that God was calling her to perfection.

This filled her heart with joy, and yet she feared. One day she happened to take up a work of St Teresa, and to find described in it graces analogous to those which she had been experiencing. (Her soul had seemed to be enclosed in God while she prayed, and she had not paid attention to a single word she had uttered.) To find this experience in St Teresa upset her altogether. She closed the book and wept with shame that she should have been so proud! for, thought she, the idea of becoming a saint often haunted her, as it had done in her childhood; she was wont to reject it as an abominable temptation to pride in a creature such as herself. 'I would have wished to be buffeted,' she cries, 'trampled under foot, rejected as impure and filthy, and yet I could not endure the least humiliation. But unhappily I carefully concealed these things which would have helped my confessor to put me on the right way.'

In 1868 Adèle's health was sufficiently re-established to let her return to her teaching, and she accepted the invitation of Madame de Crozé, an aunt of her first pupils, the young de Crochards.

chapter two

Eight Eventful Years

IT was then in 1868 that Adèle came to Aulne, where she was to spend eight eventful years. These years were to see the spoliation of the States of the Holy See, and the Pope a prisoner. They were also to see France overrun by German hordes, and bereft of the fair provinces of Alsace and Lorraine. And these outrages against all she held most dear as a Catholic and a patriot, were to be the providential means chosen by God to turn her soul towards that special vocation to which He was calling her as a victim of reparation, reparation for the crimes committed against the Church in the person of its chief Pastor, and reparation for the sins of her beloved country.

On a radiant day in spring she reached the little station of Martigné in western France, and found Madame de Crozé waiting there to meet her. With her was her little daughter Marie, then only eight years old.

Aulne must have seemed to her a rather dreary residence, hidden away in the country, far from a town, and far even from a church. Laval, the nearest town, was twenty kilometres distant, and the parish church was four. Visitors were few, and she was unable to walk even as far as the church. Yet it was here that God had called her, no doubt that in this solitude He might speak more easily to her heart.

Adèle had entire charge of the religious instruction of these happy children. She used to teach them to say their prayers with her, and then would read to them from some pious book, suited to their capacity. A good resolution for the day would be suggested to them, the whole thing lasted but five minutes. And then before they parted, each of them was taught to go and kiss with reverence the feet of a statuette of St Peter (a copy of that at Rome) which stood on Adèle's mantelpiece. They were a joyous and happy little band, and their infant piety only added to their joy. Adèle herself was always joyful and bright, though the least fatigue, even a drive in a carriage, a mere nothing, would bring on the most violent migraine.

At Aulne she was living a life to all appearance ordinary enough. But delightful companion and friend as she was, ever full of gaiety and affection, entering into all the little troubles of those around her with extraordinary tact and sympathy, there was a hidden life of the soul of which the other was but a pale reflection. One evening during the year 1869, she was in her room, when she suddenly saw appear before her a Host surrounded with rays of light, in the midst of which appeared Our Lord pointing to His Sacred Heart. She saw this vision with her bodily eyes, and it filled her with unspeakable joy. She passed that night in prayer. Later on, when she founded her Congregation, she gave to her nuns a medal to wear on their breasts, representing this vision, which was to her a never-failing source of thankful joy.

The outrages and sacrileges which Our Lord was then enduring in the person of His Vicar, the misfortunes which were now about to desolate her beloved country in the war of 1870, all this wounded her to the quick. She adored the divine Will which permitted them, but she knew that to satisfy the divine Justice there were needed offerings and sacrifices in reparation. Not only was it necessary to make satisfaction for the guilty, but to strive one's utmost to console the heart of Jesus for the insults and outrages which men made Him endure. And thus the Sacred Heart prepared her gradually for her mission of reparation.

A chapel attached to the house had long been dreamed of, and now it was decided to build it at once. The Bishop was pleased to grant to this devout family permission to have the Blessed Sacrament reserved in it, and Adèle was charged with the honour of being its Sacristan. 'Oh, what graces!' she writes, 'what hours of love and fervent prayer, in spite of the infidelities of which I was too often guilty. We had Mass at least once a week for more than a year, and then a priest came as tutor to the children, and I was given the immense consolation of daily Mass. Every morning I received Our Lord, I went to the chapel for all my spare time, and that was very often. This life was for me the ideal of happiness, until I could attain to the religious life for which I always longed, though I had no idea when or where my aspirations would be realised. I spoke of this freely to the others, in order that they might be prepared to part with me.

'However, my soul with all its fervour was active, and I no longer received from Our Lord the transports which united it so marvellously to Him in former days, nor those graces of profound recollection which separated it from all created things.

'My director, that good and holy Jesuit, always tried to turn my thoughts away from the idea of the religious life, both on account of my health and of that independent spirit which animated me in spite of myself, and which he feared would make my religious life a captivity hurtful to my soul. At the same time he assured me that he perceived in me all the possible signs of a real vocation.

'As to myself, I felt so desirous of obedience, so anxious not to lean on my own judgement, that I could not understand that independence of soul of which he spoke. Ah! I understand it now well enough. I should not have had enough courage or virtue to submit my inner life, as would have been necessary! God alone knew how I had longed and prayed for this life of love and immolation, during so many years! He, too, knew, alas! how incapable I was of living it, how unworthy to embrace it.'

chapter three

The National Vow

'THE principal object of the devotion to the Sacred Heart,' wrote St Margaret Mary, 'is to convert souls to the love of that divine Heart.' But in 1669 she received new messages which frightened her. The divine King asked that His reign should be recognised by society, that kings and princes should honour Him by a public and solemn cultus, and she, a humble cloistered nun, was to act as His messenger to the great ones of the earth. A great temple was to be built to contain the image of His Heart. That Heart willed to receive the solemn vows of the king and his whole court. He willed that His Sacred Heart should be painted on the royal standards and engraved upon the arms of the kingdom.

Louis XIV perhaps never received this message from Heaven. But when Louis XVI mounted the throne, it was hoped that his well-known piety would incline him to realise Our Lord's desire. But the storm of the Revolution soon overthrew his throne, and it was in the gloom of a prison that the unhappy king had to make his memorable vow:

'O, Jesus Christ, divine Redeemer of all our iniquities, it is in Thine adorable Heart that I would place the outpourings of my afflicted soul. I call to my help the tender Heart of Mary, my August Protectress and my Mother, and the assistance of St Louis, my patron, and the most illustrious of my ancestors.

'Be Thou opened, O adorable Heart, and receive with mercy, by the hands of those pure and powerful advocates, the vows of atonement that my confidence inspires, and that I offer to Thee as the simple expression of my feelings towards Thee. If, by the goodness of God, I recover my liberty,

'I promise...

'To go myself in person within three months from the day of my deliverance, and to pronounce on a Sunday or feast-day at the foot of the high altar, after the Offertory of the Mass, and within the hands of the Celebrant, a solemn Act of Consecration, of my person, my family and my kingdom to the Sacred Heart of Jesus, promising to give to all my subjects an example of the cultus and devotion which are due to this adorable Heart. ...

'To erect and decorate, at my own expense, a chapel or an altar to be dedicated to the Sacred Heart, which shall serve as an eternal monument of my gratitude, and of my boundless confidence in the infinite merits and in the inexhaustible treasures of grace which are enclosed in this Sacred Heart. ...

'I can to-day but pronounce in secret this engagement, but I would sign it with my blood were that necessary, and the happiest day of my life will be that on which I can publish it abroad in the temple of God. ...'

As we know, God, in His infinite and inscrutable wisdom, had other designs for this poor king. The Revolution continued its work of hate and destruction, and on January 21, 1793, he mounted the scaffold.

Almost a century elapsed and the divine wishes seemed to be completely forgotten. But in 1870 came the war with a hostile power, and soon to this were added the greater horrors of civil war. Humiliation, mourning, bloodshed, seemed to be the lot of the chosen nation. Yet an *élite* still watched and prayed.

On the morrow of the vow of Louis XVI, the army of Vendée, fighting for God and the King, wore on their breasts the image of the Sacred Heart; in 1870 the banner of that Sacred Heart made its appearance on the battle-field of Loigny. A supernatural impulse was drawing hearts in France towards the Heart of Jesus, and this appearing, as it did, spontaneously in all parts of the country, was preparing the way for the magnificent idea of the National Vow that France was to make to the Sacred Heart of her Lord.

This idea first took its rise in the city of Poitiers, and was initiated by a fervent Catholic, a Parisian, who, during the German invasion, had to take refuge there. His name was M. Legentil, and he had as his coadjutor his brother-in-law, a well-known writer, the zealous M. Rohault de Fleury. A temple was to be built which should serve as the permanent expression of the repentance and devotion of France; a temple where prayers should be ceaselessly offered up for the Sovereign Pontiff, for the Church and for France. Mgr (afterwards Cardinal) Pie, the great Bishop of Poitiers, gave the project his most cordial encouragement. Mgr Guibert, who, after the tragic death of Mgr Darboy, had been translated from the See of Tours to that of Paris, approved of it most thoroughly, and obtained for it the enthusiastic support of the entire French episcopate. Finally, Pius IX, by a brief dated July 31, 1872, gave it his supreme approbation.

The formula of the National Vow is summed up in the inscription which, later on, was engraved around the dome of the new Basilica: *Sacratissimo Cordi Jesm Gallia pœnitens et devota.*

'In view of the misfortunes which desolate France and the even greater evils which perchance still threaten her:

'In view of the sacrilegious outrages committed at Rome against the rights of the Church and of the holy See, and against the Sacred person of the Vicar of Jesus Christ:

'We humble ourselves before God, and embracing in our love both Church and Country, we confess that we have sinned and have been justly chastised:

'And in order to make reparation for our sins, and to

obtain from the infinite mercy of the Sacred Heart of Our Lord the pardon of our offences, as well as to obtain the succour necessary for the deliverance of the Sovereign Pontiff from his imprisonment and the cessations of the misfortunes of France, we promise to contribute towards the erection of a Sanctuary dedicated to the most Sacred Heart of Jesus.'

The site chosen for this votive Sanctuary was Montmartre, the Martyrs' Mount, that sacred hill of Paris which dominates the French capital. For the construction of this new church the authorisation of the civil power was necessary. The holy Archbishop of Paris, mindful of what the Sacred Heart had asked for at Paray-le-Monial, went further than this. The French Government, he pointed out, owed more than this, and must take a greater part in a work that was to be a national one. His noble audacity was amply rewarded. On July 23, 1873, after a debate in the Chamber perhaps unique in history, the National Assembly decreed by a special law, that it was of public utility to erect a monument to the Sacred Heart, and that in consequence it authorised the Archbishop of Paris to buy, even by way of expropriation, all the lands necessary, and that it recognised the Archbishops as the permanent owners of the monument.

It seems almost incredible, but so it was! The joy of the faithful can be imagined. A few months later their piety had already contributed a million francs to the work. On June 16, 1875, Cardinal Guibert, blessed the first stone of the edifice. But the construction of so great a monument must be a matter of years. So His Eminence, encouraged by the Pope, built a temporary chapel close to the site, where the faithful could already offer to the divine Heart the tribute of their supplication and their homage.

At the time of these stirring events in Catholic France, Adèle was praying in her solitude at Aulne. We will let her tell the story.

'It was in February or March, 1872, the year that I had passed in such great desolation, that I read aloud in the drawing-room an article from the *Universe,* dealing with the project of Montmartre. As I left the room to go into the garden, while I was opening the door, an inner voice said to me quite clearly, "It is there that I need thee." At the same moment I saw an altar raised on high and sparkling with lights, dominated by the Blessed Sacrament exposed in the Monstrance. I felt so overcome by this that I had to lean against the door to save myself from falling. And then I felt so happy, so happy, that I could make nothing of it. ... This memory recurred to me constantly with a ravishing sweetness, but I fancied that I was the plaything of my imagination.

'Often at night it took hold of me, at my awakening and during the course of the day it was constantly with me. This lasted eighteen months, and I could not bring myself to speak of it to Father Donnion. It was two months after his death that I found courage to tell it to Fr Chambellan. It was the feast of St Bartholomew during my confession. ... I confessed to him how this thought of being at Montmartre haunted me continually as a thing Our Saviour desired, and to which He was calling me. ... He told me to remain in peace, that it was perhaps not an illusion, and he did not forbid me to think about it in the presence of God, as long as I did not let my imagination be occupied with it.

'He asked me how I thought I could answer this call. I had not any idea, and besides, I had forbidden myself to reflect on it, fearing an illusion. Besides, there was nothing begun as yet, and it was not even certain that it would be possible to build the Basilica upon the heights of Montmartre.'

While waiting for a clearer manifestation of the divine Will, Adèle's heart was already at Montmartre. 'Often in my prayer,' she writes, 'I united myself in advance to the adorations and the reparations which were to be offered there, and always I felt that this worship would be offered to the Sacred Heart which should be continually exposed there in the Blessed Sacrament, and that there innumerable graces would flow from this inexhaustible spring on the most criminal, the most hardened of sinners; but I had no idea how I, poor I, could ever be at Montmartre.'

Though Montmartre occupied so great a place in her thoughts and prayers, Adèle was still in ignorance as to her future. She left that gladly in the hands of God. Meanwhile she continued her daily occupations.

One evening in September, 1874, she was occupied in reading the *Life of St Margaret Mary,* when suddenly this was made known to her. 'I felt Jesus speaking to my heart, illuminated by a light of surpassing brightness; He told me that it was His Will that His Heart present in the Holy Eucharist, should be the object of the worship of Montmartre, and that the Blessed Sacrament should be exposed there night and day. I was astounded at the vehemence with which Our Lord thus manifested His Will. I had had no time for reflection when I heard most distinctly these words, pronounced as it were around me. 'Go, find the Archbishop of Paris and tell him!'

'It was to me as a clap of thunder; for at that moment I was quite certain that I was receiving a formal order from my Jesus, and that I had no choice but to obey. But, alas! my cowardice and pusillanimity made me suffer a real martyrdom; and in spite of the certainty I felt in the very depth of my being, I refused to obey this command. It seemed to me too extraordinary to be really true. My resistance cost me dear. I passed the night in a state of revolt. Next morning, at Holy Communion, I think that Jesus forgave me, for I grew more calm, and I resolved to write to Fr Chambellan and tell him what had happened. He answered that it was indeed extraordinary, but that I must not show any formal resistance, to what, on the other hand, might, indeed, come from Our Lord.

'I had hoped for a formal prohibition to think any more about it. Meanwhile, I found no way out of my perplexities; nothing, no distractions, no conversations with others could make me forget it for an instant. ... Some time afterwards I saw Fr Chambellan, and after the details that I gave him, he thought that very probably I had received an order, which it was my duty to put into execution. If it were so, the matter would arrange itself.

'The months of October and November brought me no light on the problem, but no deliverance either. I knew that I should have to shoulder this burden which terrified me, and I resigned myself to it as it were by force and without any generosity.'

However, towards the end of November, Fr Chambellan took the initiative. He told her that it was not the moment to run away from duty, that her cowardice would afflict Our Saviour's Heart. She felt this herself, but she needed courage. She had no idea how to approach the Cardinal, she did not even know how to find his palace. He might refuse to see her? The Father told her that she would succeed in her mission. He had thought of giving her a letter of introduction, bearing the seal of the Company of Jesus, so that she would not be taken for an adventuress, but on the whole he thought it was better not. He therefore gave her no letter, but told her she could mention his name to the Cardinal, if that was of any use. Adèle therefore set out on her mission.

The whole thing appeared to her so unusual and so extraordinary that she would have much preferred to die, but she felt herself driven on by a superior will. When she reached Paris she wrote to ask an audience of the Cardinal. It was December 5, 1874.

Next day, after having heard Mass at the altar of the Fathers martyred during the Commune, she made a pilgrimage to Montmartre. She prayed in the old church of St Peter, for the successful achievement of the Basilica. At the moment they were preparing the foundations. Returning to her hotel, she found a letter from the Archbishop's secretary, giving her the choice of two or three days and hours for her reception by his Eminence.

On that day, December 7, after a long hour of prayer, which seemed to her a real agony, at the church of St Clotilde, she made her way to the palace, and was received by the Cardinal's private secretary. He asked her many questions, but she replied simply that it was for the Cardinal's ear alone, and eventually he introduced her into His Eminence's presence.

The Cardinal received her most kindly, but she felt very frightened. He gave her a chair beside him, and on noticing her diffidence, signed to the secretary to withdraw.

'I then said,' she tells us, 'that I thought I was obeying the Will of Our Lord in coming to tell the Archbishop of Paris that it was His desire that in the future church of the National Vow the Blessed Sacrament should be solemnly exposed night and day, and that the cult offered there should be specially directed to His Eucharistic Heart. The Cardinal replied, with a touch of irony, that this was looking a little far ahead, as the church was not yet begun. He asked me how I had been inspired to tell him this. I replied as briefly as possible, and I did not even mention the formal order of Our Lord, but only of having felt for some time an interior movement which urged me to this. He spoke to me of Fr Chambellan in the highest terms, and told me that he inspired him with great confidence, etc.

'Finally he began to speak of the devotion to the Eucharistic Heart, which he said was a novelty, and he begged me to explain what I meant by it. I was so much moved that I hardly know how I replied, but in the end he said to me: "Then you think, my child, that it is specially to the Heart of Jesus in the Blessed Sacrament that the worship of Montmartre should be addressed?" I replied, "Yes, your Eminence, and it is for that reason that Our Lord desires that the Blessed Sacrament should be exposed there day and night." The Cardinal replied that that did not appear to be possible. However, he had the kindness to tell me of his plans for the Basilica, of his hopes and desires, and then he gave me his blessing, and showed me out by another way so that I should not have to meet the secretary.

'Deeply moved, and in absolute ignorance whether my act of obedience to Our Lord would, or would not, have any result in the future, I went to a church to thank Our Saviour for having been my support, and then returned to my lodging in order to write to Fr Chambellan an account of what had passed. On the following day, the feast of the Immaculate Conception, I went to Notre Dame des Victoires, and next day, December 9, returned to Madame de Crozé's château to continue my ordinary occupations. Not long afterwards I met Fr Chambellan, who considered that Our Lord had certainly helped me through the affair. And he said that I was not to worry about the result; I had done what Jesus wanted, and all was well.'

More than fifty years have passed since this memorable interview. We do not know what impression it made on the Cardinal, but we do know the result. We know the splendid realisation of the message Our Lord sent by Adèle, his humble confidante. We know that for more than forty years the solemn Exposition of the Blessed Sacrament has never ceased at Montmartre, night and day, even during the great war when the enemies' shells were threatening to destroy the white Basilica of the Sacred Heart. And it was Cardinal Guibert himself, who established, first in the temporary chapel, then in the Basilica of the Vow, this perpetual adoration that seemed so impossible a few years before. The ardour and generosity of his people triumphed over the hesitations of the Pontiff. 'This is the Lord's doing, and it is marvellous in our eyes.'

The first trial of these night watches began on March 3, 1881; the fifth anniversary of the opening of the temporary chapel, and it was decisive. On August 1, 1885, the Adoration became perpetual, and since then Our Lord has never left His Eucharistic Throne, save to give His Benediction to those who come to visit Him.

But what was to be Adèle's own part in this great work? It would appear that in her vision of Montmartre she saw not only the Blessed Sacrament exposed, but herself kneeling there in the midst of a crowd of souls devoted to the work of reparation. About a year subsequent to her visit to Cardinal Guibert, she was inspired, with the permission of her director, to write the following letter to the Archbishop of Paris:

'...While at Montmartre the Sanctuary where Jesus wills to receive with all the love of His Heart the prayers and supplications of the whole of France is in course of erection, it would no doubt be pleasing to this divine Master to see the work of national reparation have a beginning in retreat and silence, by means of a living sanctuary composed of souls in the religious state specially and uniquely consecrated to this cult of reparation towards His adorable Heart, which is so constantly being outraged in the most Blessed Sacrament. In this France, which He loves, and where He has been pleased to manifest the torrents of love and mercy of which the Holy Eucharist is at once the ocean and the channel, does He not expect to find souls, objects of His special mercy, uniting themselves to Him, consecrating themselves for ever to the prayer of reparation at the foot of His altar, and obtaining by their humble supplications a slackening of the sacrileges committed against Him, and a check to the contagious temptations of indifference and neglect? ...

'Your Eminence may perhaps ask yourself who am I who thus venture to make such supplication. Indeed, I am the least and most unworthy of the creatures who are the objects of God's infinite grace; but I make no resistance to this spirit of love and reparation which for several years past has taken possession of my life, and which impels me to-day thus to address myself to your Eminence. It was the same spirit, my Lord, which last year led me to your feet to beg you to be good enough to think seriously of establishing at the church of the Sacred Heart a convent of religious devoted to the work of reparation. If the apparent strangeness of this proceeding has left any remembrance of it in the mind of your Eminence, deign to pardon me for it as well as for this one. ... And if it should seem good to you, that the Heart of Jesus should be glorified by the realisation of the petition that I now make, may your Eminence deign to summon me and to question me, to assure yourself of the reality of a call, which for the last three years is appealing with an ever-growing force and persistence... yes, even if I have to receive from the interview nothing but confusion and humiliation. The Beloved Master who has taken possession of my soul wills to reign therein without rival and has by His powerful grace planted there the spirit of resignation to His divine Will.

'I think that I ought to make known to your Eminence that in all these actions and steps which I have thought it my duty to take, I have never acted without the permission of my director, who alone knows the mercies of the Lord in my behalf and the aspirations of my soul. If your Eminence considers that there is nothing serious in all this, it means that Our Lord does not will the realisation of the desires with which He seems to have inspired me. In that case, as at present, I will bless Him and love Him, without undue astonishment at His inscrutable Will.'

Six-and-twenty years were yet to elapse before the realisation of the work first asked of her in 1872. Years of multiplied graces for this chosen soul, but also years of suffering, of abandonment to the Will of God, of heroic confidence.

chapter four

First Sojourn At Montmartre

THE year 1876 saw not only the laying of the first stone of the Basilica, but also the opening of the temporary chapel at Montmartre. It became at once the goal of innumerable pilgrimages, from France, and from every part of the Christian world.

And now Adèle's desire to make it her home became more and more ardent. A new idea took possession of her soul. She pictured herself living at Montmartre, in solitude. There she saw herself spending all her free time before the Tabernacle in adoration, living for that alone, as a victim set apart for sacrifice. 'It all seemed to me strange, impossible, mad,' she says, 'but Jesus assured me that such was His Will for me, and that He would bring it to pass. I told it all to Fr Chambellan.'

It was to be the first station of her long way of the Cross. The Father heard her, but gave no decision. He had, as a prudent director, to be assured that such was really the Will of God. He wanted proofs. There were many obvious objections. How could her weak health support the austerities of an eremetical life? Was it not an act of imprudence thus to separate herself from family and friends? What would happen to her in case of sickness? Adèle did not possess the necessary resources to sustain life, how would she find them there?

But her health grew better every day, so that those around her were astounded at the change. The Father had also stipulated that Adèle must have a companion with her. God provided one. Adèle herself yearned for a life completely solitary, but here she had to give way. A young lady of Laval, who was devoted to her, offered herself as a companion. As to her family, Adèle wrote to her sisters and told them of her project, and their answers filled her with thankfulness and joy. They quite understood her motives, and promised to do all they could to make her project feasible. Their reply made a great impression on the Father, but he still hesitated.

He had another obviously prudent condition to make. Adèle, while at Montmartre, must be in touch with some religious Community of the neighbourhood, which could, in case of need, serve her as a shelter and a support. This was difficult, as she hardly knew Paris, and was not acquainted with any Community there. Besides, there must be someone in this convent who had experience in the supernatural dealings of God with favoured souls and who would understand Adèle and her desires, and would take an interest in them.

Adèle herself writes: 'I counted on God's goodness, and I was not disappointed. Towards the middle of February, 1876, the eldest of my little pupils, who had suffered in her eyes for some time, now grew worse, and as her parents were prevented by important matters from accompanying her to Paris, to consult a specialist, they begged me to be her companion. Madame de Crozé asked me to find a Community with whom we could stay, and told me she had heard that the nuns of Marie Reparatrice would take in boarders who had proper testimonials. Through my friend the Superior of these nuns at Le Mans, I obtained an introduction to their house at Paris, at 21 Rue de Calais. They agreed to take us in for a week. On consulting a map of Paris, during our journey in the train, I found that the Rue de Calais was situated at the foot of the hill of Montmartre.' Here was the hand of God!

They were kindly welcomed at the Convent, where they arrived just before Benediction. They were taken to the chapel at once, and thus Our Lord seemed to bid them welcome. They passed a nun on the staircase who silently saluted them. 'If she were the Superior,' thought Adèle, 'how easily I could open my heart to her, it seems to me that she would understand.' Mother

Marie de St Louis de Gonzague was, in fact, the Superior of the Convent, and was to prove the support and stay that was needed. She was one of the first Sisters to join the Congregation of Marie Reparatrice, and she gave to it her devoted services for more than fifty years.

During the week they spent at the Convent, Adèle spent most of her time in prayer. She felt still more strongly the irresistible attraction towards Montmartre. She prayed with all her soul that she might conform her will entirely to the divine Will, and that Our Lord would enlighten her director, so that his decision should be the expression of that Will. She says that as she passed the little house, No. 46 Rue de la Fontenelle (now Rue de la Barre), she felt quite sure that that was where she should stay, but she attached no importance to the matter. At the future chapel she offered herself once more as a victim, with deep emotion, and with the sure hope that God's mercy would accept her sacrifice.

On their return to Aulne, she anxiously awaited March 3, when her director had promised to make known to her his decision. She had almost given up hope of hearing it, when a letter was put into her hands, which had been mislaid in the post. She read in it that Fr Chambellan gave her his permission and even his fatherly encouragement to undertake the mission to which she felt herself called. He gave her a month for the necessary arrangements.

The hardest part was to make known to these beloved friends, under whose roof she had spent eight memorable and happy years, that she must now leave them. They were inconsolable, and Adèle herself was almost broken-hearted at their grief. But she felt herself so upheld by the knowledge of God's Will, that she never faltered. Her future companion, she found, could not leave for some months, but for this delay she could only thank Our Lord, for she felt in her inmost heart that she ought to be alone. Her director allowed her to leave two months before her companion could join her. Then there was the question of the lodging. Here, too, she was providentially assisted. A devout lady of her acquaintance was just about to leave for Paris, to spend her Easter with her daughter. She wrote to her on Maundy Thursday, telling her of her project, begging her to find a suitable lodging in a modest house near the Chapel of the Sacred Heart. On Easter Sunday she got her reply; enclosing the receipt for the first quarter's rent. It was the very house which had attracted her notice, No. 46 Rue de la Fontenelle.

The last days at Aulne were naturally very sad. On May 1, Adèle left this dear home, never to see it again. She went to Poitiers, after a short visit to Laval, and there made a week's retreat under the guidance of Fr Chambellan. On May 16 she arrived at Paris to begin her solitary life there. She was welcomed at the Convent of Marie Reparatrice. The Superior was more than kind, and Adèle gave her a letter from Fr Chambellan confiding her to the Reverend Mother's maternal care and placing her under her obedience. She at once made her way up the hill to visit the temporary chapel, now completed. She got there just in time for Benediction, and remained there till the doors were closed for the night. She was filled with joy and thankfulness.

On returning to the Convent, the Reverend Mother said that she should remain a few days with her there, but go to Montmartre each day. Next day she went back there, and visited her lodging, the two little attics at No. 46. Her friend, Madame d'Evry, who had given her the keys at Laval, had prepared everything for her. Even the bed was made. There was a crucifix on the wall, and pictures of the Sacred Heart, Our Lady and St Joseph. Everything necessary was there, even a little store of provisions. Filled with gratitude, she longed more than ever to remain there. Next day this was granted her, and after supper, she was allowed to go to sleep in her little Nazareth, hard by the Sacred Heart. Next morning she awoke with a heart bursting with thankful joy. It was the anniversary of her First Communion, and it was also the day of her first Communion at Montmartre.

'I offered myself to Jesus without reservation, asking Him to take me as a victim, either by taking away my life, as I desired, or by making it entirely consecrated to His good pleasure, without leaving me the least personal satisfaction. From this moment, I felt myself absolutely separated from the world. ... All the morning was filled with happiness and thanksgiving.'

But this happiness was soon to give way to the bitter agony of Satanic assaults. She describes the martyrdom she went through. For hours the excess of her suffering nailed her down, she could not move, she only longed to die. She found that even that desire became impossible, for it seemed to her that she was damned, and forsaken by God. She passed all that night in agony, without a ray of hope or consolation, yet she was still able to resign herself to the Will of God. Next morning she found that she could not stand upright or move her feet. Not till the evening was she able to go downstairs. She wrote to her director that it seemed clear that she had been tempting God, that He had abandoned her, that she would die if He willed it, but that she could not remain at Montmartre.

She returned with the greatest difficulty to the Convent, and asked for the Mother Superior. Adèle looked at her with consternation and despair, and faltered out: 'Mother, this is above my strength, I cannot return to Montmartre, or I shall certainly die there.' 'Well,' she said, 'then you will die, it will be quite simple; and you are going to return there this evening. I will give you some supper, and then you will go back. I order you to. To-morrow, if you feel more brave, you will return here at midday. I will pray for you, and Our Lord will protect you against the snares of the Evil One, for it is he who is striving to make you renounce the call to which Jesus has inspired you.'

These words were like a flash of light to her, and though still very unhappy, she was able again to place all her confidence in God. She ate something by obedience, and then returned, as it were to martyrdom. In the night she suffered as never before in all her life. But her will, once thus enlightened, never faltered. She accepted everything and consented to suffer everything, rather than leave the spot to which she knew Our Lord had called her. She was able, though still suffering terribly, to hear Mass in the chapel, and make her Communion. At midday she returned to the Convent, more dead than alive.

The Reverend Mother received her with the utmost kindness, and told her that the conflict through which she had passed, and which was not yet finished, had a great importance; and that when she saw her the evening before she had immediately understood that she was enduring a violent assault from the powers of hell, and that it was necessary at any cost that she should gain the victory. She said that she had passed the whole night in prayer for Adèle, and that she had felt that the rage of hell was being turned against herself, but she rejoiced at that, for she believed that Our Lord would be greatly glorified by this victory. Adèle felt that this good Mother was to her an Angel of Consolation, and the messenger of the Holy Ghost.

She continued to suffer acutely, but the certainty that she was doing the Will of God was an enormous support and consolation. Calm followed the storm; and the victim began to give herself with a complete abandonment into the hands of the sacrificing Priest. In this life of solitude at Montmartre Adèle found peace, serenity and joy. She experienced many wonderful graces from the divine Providence that watched over her. Even in material needs she had proof that she was not forgotten.

This dying to self was being rapidly consummated. In the course of July her health became weaker, and the Mother Superior obliged her to take more care of herself. The great heat of her little lodging, a low attic under the roof, caused her much suffering. But this was nothing to the pains she suffered in her soul, which only gave her a little respite during the hours of Mass, when she received graces that gave her courage to endure. Little by little her life became a martyrdom, the very remembrance of which in later years made her tremble. She thought she was lost, she saw no possible means of appeasing the justice of God. Her life, as she says herself, became a very hell.

Nevertheless, all this time one light remained to her, and though without sensible consolation, it enabled her to accept her state without reserve. It came to her from a chapter in the *Imitation of Christ* (Book IV, Ch. 8), the chapter on the Oblation of Christ. Every time she read it, this light was given her, and for an instant she saw clearly, and was given the strength to continue to suffer. She could not read anything else, and even that only once a day.

Her health grew weaker every day. If she tried to sweep out her little room, she fell down. When going up or down stairs, she was seized by a vertigo, which obliged her to sit down to rest several times; in fact, she felt she was dying. Not that she feared to die, she desired it with all her heart. One day she heard Our Lord saying within her heart: 'I did not bring thee here that thou shouldst take root here, that will be only in Heaven. Go forward then, as Abraham did, until I show thee the place of thy last sacrifice.'

On August 23 the crisis came. She could hardly drag herself to the chapel, and when she tried to leave it after Mass, she found she could not move. Some charitable souls who were there, half carried her, half dragged her home. They laid her on her bed and she begged them to let the Superior of Marie Reparatrice know how ill she was. They at once sent a lay-sister to nurse her. They summoned a doctor, who could make nothing of her state. She had a telegram sent to her young friend at Laval, who came the next day. That evening she tried to get up for a moment, but she fainted away. For some days her illness became more and more serious. In the evening of August 30, the doctor said there was no more hope, and it was a question of the Last Sacraments. After receiving these, she became a little better.

A day or two later her sister arrived, charged by her father to bring her home as soon as she could be moved. After a few days she was pronounced out of danger, but she could not get up, or even speak more than a few words. But though the danger of death was past, it was evident that a still greater sacrifice was demanded of her. She longed to die, but it would break her heart to leave her beloved Montmartre while she was still alive. Yet it was clearly necessary. She wrote to her friend: 'Fiat! Fiat! I can only feel the happiness of being thus the plaything of His adorable Will. Does He intend to send me away? It seems to me impossible to believe this. On the other hand, is it not tempting God to continue a life which cannot be borne save by miracle? Ask the good Master to do with me what He wills. Father Chambellan will decide my fate.'

The departure was fixed for September 15. One of the Fathers of the Oblates of Mary Immaculate, who had been her Confessor, Fr Giroux, got leave to bring her the day before as a supreme consolation, the Blessed Sacrament from the temporary chapel at Montmartre. It was the first time that Our Lord had left this chapel.

chapter five

The Reparation

SHE returned to her home at Dijon with her sister Marie. Her old father was quite overcome at the sight of her suffering. The doctors seemed to be unable to do anything. Yet, as she told her friend, she was happy in spite of everything, for God had decided it all, and she had nothing to do but obey and to pronounce her *fiat*. She had no anxieties, because she knew she was in the hands of her Jesus. Her sister occupied herself with her spiritual needs, and before long, a young priest from the Cathedral of St Benigne brought her Holy Communion every week.

In November she had fresh sufferings, indeed, she thought that she was going mad. Despair seemed to fill her soul. But the Immaculate Mother of God came to her aid on December 8, her feast day, and all her sufferings disappeared, as it were, miraculously, and she was filled with divine consolations. But these only lasted during the Octave of the Feast, it was but an oasis in the appalling wilderness of her tribulations. Gradually her health improved, during December she was able to get up and to walk a little; at Christmas she was actually able to assist at the Midnight Mass. But things grew worse again after the Epiphany, and on January 7, there began for her poor soul and body a new martyrdom which lasted seven months.

She often thought that she was at the point of death; but far more terrible than her bodily sufferings were the agonies her soul endured. She wrote of this time: 'The thought of this terrible trial can never be effaced from my memory. I could not understand how a human creature could possibly support it. The feeling of my pitiable state never quitted me, I bore all the weight of it with immense agony. I used to say with heart and lips, "My God, Thy will be done," that was my only prayer, I could not then say even a whole *Paternoster*.'

In March it was decided that the only hope was to send her to take the waters at Alise Sainte Reine in the Côte-d'Or, and her sister went with her. Fr Chambellan encouraged her by letters. Yes, if the Heart of Jesus wished for her recovery, all was well. But if He preferred to leave the victim on the cross, hanging between life and death, He knew that her will was His, and that she would thank Him for keeping her in this state to which His love had called her. Her devoted young friend from Laval came to join her at Ste. Reine and was so much touched by the sight of her sufferings that she entreated her to let her take her to Lourdes. Adèle left the decision to her director, who encouraged her to consent. 'And if divine grace draws you to ask for your cure, then do it with all the fervour of your heart,' he added.

The journey was very painful, but Adèle found it very consoling. It took them eight days, and her young friend feared more than once that she was going to die in her arms. But at last they reached Lourdes safely on the Vigil of the Feast of the Assumption. A priest she encountered on the way told her she would not be cured, because she did not really want it, and she arrived at Lourdes in what seemed to be a dying state. However, next morning she was carried to the Basilica, and thence to the Grotto. She writes: 'I could not ask for my cure, that was quite impossible, unless it was for the honour of the Blessed Virgin. But I did ask for enough strength to enable me to go to Mass and Holy Communion every morning, even if I have to suffer a martyrdom the rest of the time.' However, she found herself distinctly better after she had been plunged in the healing waters, and at the moment that they left Lourdes this improvement became much more marked, so that they were able to travel back to her home at Dijon in four days. To her regret, when she got home, she found that this improvement was attributed to the baths at Ste Reine, rather than to the waters of Lourdes.

The doctors, who found her health much improved, now decided to send her to Brittany, where her sister Joséphine was teaching, at Bruz, not far south of Rennes. Near the house where her sister was living was a little home for the aged, and here the sisters in charge received her gladly as a boarder. She was given a large room that, to her great joy, opened into the sanctuary of the chapel, so that every morning the chaplain brought her Holy Communion from the altar during Mass. She loved to think that, in her bed, she was so close to the tabernacle and that she could assist at the offices, just as if she were actually in the chapel. At Benediction she was even nearer to the Monstrance than was the priest himself. Adèle remained in this refuge until December, 1878. She was very happy there and was visited every day by her devoted sister. Her health gradually improved, though she was still very weak.

She had intended to return home to Dijon, but her young friend from Laval begged her so earnestly to remain, that she consented, and stayed there two years and a half. She found her numerous visitors there very trying, and still more the excessive affection of her friend. She says that she felt herself incapable of thought or of prayer, and could only make acts of resignation to the divine Will. But her friends and acquaintances thought quite differently. They came in crowds to see her, to enjoy the charm of her conversation and to consult her as to their spiritual difficulties. Meanwhile she was growing a little stronger, and she helped her friend in her occupation of embroidering church vestments by making the designs for them. She was extremely artistic all her life, and drew most beautifully.

Meanwhile, Fr Chambellan, at that time Provincial of the Jesuits, who were now undergoing persecution, had left France for Canterbury, where the Fathers had obtained the property known as Hales Place. On May 1, 1881, Adèle had the happiness of meeting her whole family at Dijon. It was the first time for ten years that such a family reunion had taken place. They had all grieved to find how poorly their aged father was, and since they could not hope to have him with them much longer, they had decided to spend the month of May beneath his roof. Their principal preoccupation was the state of his soul, for he had not practised his religion for many years. They had prayed most earnestly for him all these years, and Adèle at her first Communion had offered her life for him. But he gave no sign of any change. The priest, M. Bizouard, who had been wont to bring Adèle Holy Communion, used to visit him. He always received him kindly and seemed grateful for his visits, but that was all.

On May 18, when Adèle was too suffering to leave her bed, his doctor came to see her, and she begged him to tell her plainly what he thought of her father's state. The family, she said, was determined to do anything rather than allow him to die without the last Sacraments. The doctor told her that there was no time to be lost, indeed, he thought it was a question only of days before the end. Yet the old man still refused to rest, he would try and go out-of-doors, he was constantly coming into Adèle's room to enquire after her health, he was intensely grieved at her sufferings. He seemed to suffer from nothing but extreme restlessness, and he could not even remain in his bed at night. They sent for the priest, who could only come the following day. Meanwhile, divine grace was evidently at work in his soul. He kept saying, 'Children, pray for me!' Adèle used to answer: 'Father, pray yourself with me.' 'I can't,' he said, 'but I do pray sometimes. I feel I am going; that I shall be no longer here on Sunday.'

Adèle, however, got him to say with her some words of prayer, just like a little child. Next day, May 19, the priest came, and it was manifest that divine grace had conquered. He found the old man in the best possible dispositions, and really anxious to make his confession. It was difficult, as his mind was beginning to wander, but he did his best, and the priest was perfectly satisfied. He promised to bring him Holy Viaticum next morning, if his state permitted him to receive It. He gave him Extreme Unction then and there, while he was in full consciousness, and was doing his best to pray with all his heart. His tears, his efforts to pray, his humble gratitude for the grace that had been vouchsafed to him, were an immense consolation to his children. After the priest's departure, one of his daughters suggested to him acts of contrition, of faith, hope and charity, and other prayers, the old man meanwhile kissing his crucifix with many tears. But an hour later he had lost consciousness, and the agony began.

Adèle's consolation at her father's return to God after so many years may be imagined. It was an additional joy to her to think that this grace had been granted to him on that very day, May 19, the anniversary of her first Communion, when she had offered her life for his conversion. The following day this beloved father expired in the arms of one of his daughters.

After their father's death they left the old house, and went to live in the square of St Benigne, close to the Cathedral, which until the Revolution had been a Benedictine Abbey. She could now walk a little, and about twice a week they were able to take her to Mass, and Holy Communion. In the spring of 1885, she was able to go there every other day, and at the end of April even every day, often by herself. From that day, she says, her life became more interior, more for God alone. ... The spirit of prayer developed in her soul with an intensity that she had never yet known (save at Montmartre) even at the time of her first fervour. The time given to her prayers fortified her soul for the rest of the day, and she was ever longing after it. At the same time she obtained the grace to bear with joy the trouble and difficulties of her daily life. From time to time her soul seemed to be so plunged and lost in God, that she was no longer conscious of her surroundings.

chapter six

The Mystic Espousals

THE year 1887 was destined to mark a period of transition in Adèle's spiritual life. The divine Heart that was forming her in His own image began to show her more and more clearly the path she had to follow. The way of abandonment, of surrender, which she had so long followed, now becomes more distinct than ever. She has now no will but the divine Will, it is her unique preoccupation, and she follows it with the more joy when it calls her to a self-crucifixion of her whole being.

The Abbé Courtois, a very holy priest of the diocese, was chaplain at this time of the Carmelite nuns at Dijon. He was well qualified to guide Adèle on the road Our Lord was marking out for her. With the full approval of her director, Adèle became the penitent of this holy priest, and she was destined to remain under his guidance until his death in 1892. One of his first acts was to oblige her to relate to him in writing all the principal graces of her life, and it is to this that we owe so many precious details of God's dealings with her soul.

Adèle had already, in 1873, consecrated herself entirely to the Heart of Our Lord in the most Holy Eucharist. But that did not satisfy her thirst for immolation. On June 17, 1887, she made, with the permission of her director, a vow of complete abandonment. 'Henceforth,' she says, 'I shall consider myself as a little trifle given to Jesus, and immolated as an absolute holocaust, without ever being able to reclaim it.' She asked of God, in words that throw much light upon her soul, to glorify Himself in her without her knowing it herself. After making this vow, she seems to have experienced a new life. She says that Jesus now watched over her like a mother teaching her little one to walk.

On November 2 of this year, another great grace is offered to her. She had offered the day, in union with the Church, for the Holy Souls in Purgatory, and it had been a day of continual suffering. In the evening she was absolutely tired out. But she did not shrink from asking for more suffering, if that was the divine Will. Then she began to make the act of abandonment in these words: 'Heart of my Jesus, I offer and abandon myself entirely to Thee, in the spirit of obedience and also of love, even though I feel it not.' These words were scarcely uttered when Adèle found herself suddenly ravished by the ineffable Vision of the Adorable Trinity. She felt herself actually in contact with the Triune God. And a divine light showed her that this grace was accorded to her by virtue of the Sacred Humanity of our Saviour. Then almost without realising it, she cried out in the midst of the ravishing happiness that seemed to crush her, 'My Jesus, what dost Thou want?' and then, in the midst of an outpouring of light ineffable and of divine harmony, she heard the reply which, she says, made more impression on her soul than any grace she had yet received, 'To espouse thee.'

On the morrow, when the priest was giving her Communion, she distinctly heard the voice of the Beloved say to her: 'This is the Feast of our Betrothal.' 'My thanksgiving began with an offering of adoration, which Jesus Himself inspired in my soul. Then all at once I saw Him seated on a throne of light in the midst of an immense hall. He was surrounded by a great company of virgin souls, His brides, beautiful, shining with purity and love, crowned, and, I believe, each bearing, like Him, a sceptre in the right hand. As to me, I hid myself in the furthest corner of this immense hall. Jesus came to me and formed around me by His sole Will, as it were, a dark chamber, and He said to me: "Thou wilt remain there, and I will come to visit thee, and I will Myself prepare thee to be My bride." In my heart I said to Him: "But, Lord, I do nothing for Thee." He answered: "Thou hast but to let me work in thee, it is for this reason that I asked of thee the vow of abandonment." '

Adèle remained then in her prison. There was neither fire nor light there. She felt no love, she did not understand what was passing, but she waited in peace the visit of her Lord who had promised Himself to prepare her to become His bride. 'It seemed to me,' she says, 'that His desire was to see me clothed in the modest virtues of patience, gentleness, kindness, humility and self-denial. I saw clearly that for this He asked of me only a great fidelity to His guidance, and I promised Him to do my best.'

On November 14 Adèle related to her confessor the wonderful grace that had been granted to her. While the priest gave to her the Sacred Host, she distinctly heard within her soul these words: 'This is the Marriage.' Troubled for an instant, she dared not swallow the Host. 'At last,' she writes, 'Jesus descended within me, as I returned to my place. As I bent down humbly to adore Him, something most marvellous happened to me, and even now I tremble with joy every time I think of it. I found myself, as it were, stretched out upon the cross, crucified with Jesus so that I was as it were fused, transformed into Him; only those who have experienced it will understand what I mean. ... Having never experienced anything of the kind before, and not understanding what was passing within me, I said to Our Lord: "Oh, my God, what does it mean, what art Thou doing? (O mon Dieu, que se passe-t-il? Que faites-Vous?)" "I take possession of thee, thou art My spouse," was the reply. This was followed by such interior caresses, such a taking possession of my soul by the Heavenly Bridegroom, that I felt in all reality that I lost all liberty, all power over myself. ... And then there appeared before me, or within me, I know not which, the Face of my Jesus crowned with thorns. But this vision was like a flash of lightning and seemed to last no longer. I knelt down, for the moment of the Elevation was approaching, and just as the priest raised on high the Sacred Victim, I saw again my Jesus, but now in the glory of His risen life. He seemed to be veiled by a light cloud, so that I could only faintly perceive Him. This vision lasted only during the Elevation, and immediately after it, I saw the Blessed Virgin presenting to me the Infant Jesus standing upright beside her. He stretched out His arms to me, and smiled on me, and Mary also smiled, but a sort of transparent cloud was veiling them a little. This vision lasted perhaps one minute.'

A little later, Adèle was wondering how such inexplicable things could happen to one like her, and then she heard the interior voice saying to her: 'This day have I espoused thee in the Faith.' Then she asked Him as a proof that He was, indeed, the author of these mysterious happenings to grant her the grace of dying of love for Him. He replied: 'I will grant thee this, proof.' She then had the thought that this would be granted to her only in the next world, but she heard Him reply to the thought: 'To die of love is to live for love of Me, dost thou not understand?'

At another time He vouchsafed to her this light on the subject of the Mystic Espousals. 'It is truly the Word of God who becomes the Spouse of the soul He has chosen, and this is the manner of it. In His Incarnation He has espoused human nature by means of His Sacred Humanity, and it is by means of this intimate link which is formed between His Blessed Soul and certain chosen ones, that they are called to become by participation the brides of the Word. This marvellous favour, which none can merit, but which Jesus grants to whom He wills, is nevertheless not granted save to souls who have a special devotion to His Sacred Humanity.'

During November, 1887, Adèle, at His invitation, began to rise during the night in order to pray for the Church, the Holy Father, and the clergy – and during this time He deigned to command her to consecrate herself entirely to His Will. He Himself inspired her thus to offer herself to Him. 'I unite myself to Jesus and I consecrate myself to the divine Will, for the Church, the Pope and the Clergy – I submit myself with all my heart to all that this adorable Will shall do in me and by me.'

Every day, she was told, she was to renew this consecration of her will before the Blessed Sacrament. 'I said to Him, "But, dear Lord, what if I forget?" "Well, I shall not be offended," He replied.' She was not to be afraid that she was called to bear a cross too heavy for her strength – He would act in her. He told her, too, that she could continue to pray and to offer herself for the special intentions to which she felt drawn, but in a general manner; and little by little she understood that her consecration to the needs of the Church, the Pope and the clergy, contained in itself all the intentions to which she felt herself drawn.

Her devotion to the Sacred Liturgy was always very marked; she felt that she could not better honour the most Holy Trinity than by uniting herself to the sacrifice of the Incarnate Word on our altars. She expresses it thus: 'As the Mass begins, I recollect myself and place myself in the presence of God, without feeling any great fervour – I humble myself before God, thanking Him for my poverty, my misery, which oblige me to have recourse simply and solely to Him. Then, showing to Him His divine Son, the adorable Victim who is about to offer Himself in the Holy Sacrifice, I offer Him myself, as an adorer worthy of Him, an adorer infinitely adorable as He is Himself – it seems to me, then, that I see the Holy Spirit as the ineffable union of this Father and this Son, and contemplate in this Holy Trinity the sole truth, the sole beauty, and the sole love.

'Having thus, as it were, in my possession, our divine Lord, and offering Him to His Father to adore Him, praise Him, thank Him, supplicate Him, and love Him perfectly, I put no bounds to my desires, to my entreaties; all for the glory of God, all submitted joyously to His good pleasure. Then I remain plunged in contemplation, remembering no more my supplications, nor any creature, nor any work for God; but having cast all my solicitudes on Jesus, in order that He may present them to His Father, I forget myself entirely, and gaze simply upon the Adorable Trinity.' And thus Our Lord deigned to call her to share in His priesthood.

chapter seven

The Last Years Before
The Foundation

ADÈLE returned to Dijon in 1881, a little before her father's death; and there she continued to live with her sisters, Marie and Joséphine. Their brother Victor spent with them his periods of leave (he was a naval engineer), while the eldest sister, Louise, lived with a cousin at Avot in the Côte d'Or. In the spring of 1892, Marie's state of health obliged the sisters to leave Dijon for the country. They went at first to Alise Sainte Reine, on account of its bracing air. It was a great sacrifice to Adèle to leave Dijon, where she had received such marvellous graces, and to be separated from the confessor to whom she had rendered so faithful an account of them. But she had, as she told him, the consolation of having yet another sacrifice to offer to her Lord, and this gave her strength.

Here it was, at last, that Adèle had the happiness of meeting her who was to become her first disciple and daughter, her chief collaborator and assistant in the work to which she was called, her second self, as it were, and her most devoted companion. This was Alice Andrade, afterwards to be known as Mother Agnes of the Sacred Heart, Co-Foundress of the Congregation, and successor of Adèle as its Mother-General. Her father, M. Michel Andrade, was an old college friend of Adèle's brother Victor. They were both naval engineers, and were devoted to one another. Her mother was English, and they had first met at Cherbourg.

Alice was born there January 20, 1873, and was only a baby when her mother died. In 1879 M. Andrade married again, a young lady who became a true mother to the little orphan, and during the next ten years the family circle was enlarged by the birth of three sons and two more daughters. Unhappily, to please the English mother, little Alice was brought up as a Protestant, though all the rest of the family were good Catholics. It is true she went to school at a convent, but she was taken regularly for religious instruction to a Protestant Pastor, and she frequented the services at his meeting-house. She was, however, from the first, a Catholic at heart, and she longed to become one in reality. At last, when she was sixteen years old, she was, after many prayers, permitted by her father to abjure Protestantism and to be received into the one true Church of Christ.

From that day she devoted herself to a most fervent Catholic life. She seems to have had even then some foretaste of the life to which God was calling her. She organised among her companions a sort of religious community, with its rule, its practices of piety, its penances and mortifications, and all this was most faithfully observed.

But above all, she was always joyful, and she saw most things in a comic light. Nevertheless, she had, but a little time after her conversion, to pass (like so many souls destined to great holiness) through a real torment of scruples. She had constantly to have recourse to her confessor to bring peace to her tortured soul. Happily she had the grace to practise absolute obedience, and thus this trial, though prolonged, only helped her to advance in the way of the Cross.

Another difficulty she experienced was the doubt as to her true vocation. For a long time she sought to know God's will for her, without receiving any clear response. The sudden death of her father (in October, 1893), when she was approaching her twenty-first year, was destined to enlighten her soul. It was a most terrible blow to her, but it helped her to see her way. She used to speak of it as the 'Ransom of the Beloved,' and her desire was now fixed to consecrate herself to God in order to save the soul of the father she loved, who had been taken from her so suddenly by a fatal accident.

She had already confided to him her desires for a religious life, and he had made no opposition to the project, though the prospect of parting from this beloved child was extremely painful to him. But she was not attracted to any Community that she knew. She did, indeed, try her vocation with the teaching sisters of the Order of St Dominic, but a month was sufficient to show her that it was not there that God would have her. She had, too, an inner conviction that God meant her to take part in a new foundation, but she had no idea how she was to set about it.

It was Joséphine Garnier who was destined to solve the problem. She came to Paris in 1896, and her brother, who feared that the death of his old comrade, M. Andrade, might have left the family badly off (though this was not the case), had urged her to offer to the widow and children a home for the summer months in their house at Villeneuve. Joséphine soon became great friends with the Andrades, and she was specially drawn to Alice, in whom she recognised unusual gifts. She soon divined her trouble, and before long she was able to suggest to her the means by which she might find the road to which God seemed to be drawing her. They were out for a walk together one day when Alice felt herself moved to confide in this new friend her hopes of some day taking part in a religious foundation. But she felt that the whole idea seemed so presumptuous, that it was very hard for her to speak of it. It was not, indeed, until they were almost home again that she armed herself with all her courage, and suddenly blurted out, as it were: 'The reason why I don't get married, is that I believe that I am destined to take part in a foundation, where there will be continual prayer for the Church and the Pope, but I do not know of any such foundation.'

Joséphine's surprise and delight can be imagined, she at once began to tell her, discreetly, something of the work to which her sister Adèle felt herself called by the Sacred Heart: and when she reached the house she at once wrote to Adèle:

'If it is God's will that you begin the work to which you feel He is calling you, I think that I have found you your first companion.' At last the holiday season began, and the Andrades set out for Villeneuve. 'The very evening of our arrival,' wrote Alice some years later, 'we all went to dine with the Misses Garnier. They were waiting for us on the lawn. Immediately I saw our mother, I flung myself into her arms, crying out, "My mother!" "My daughter!" she replied; and from that moment I had not the slightest doubt that I was called to be with her.'

Thus began a union which only death was to sever, and that but for a little while! Adèle opened her heart to the young companion whom God had so manifestly given to her, and together they discussed their future life in all its details. Adèle had, indeed, no idea of becoming the foundress. This place of honour, she trusted, was reserved for another, a lady of great piety who seemed to be well fitted for a part from which she herself shrank. There were two or three others of whom she had hopes. When the Andrades had to return to Paris in October, for the beginning of the school year, there began between the 'mother' and 'daughter' a long and intimate correspondence, which is still preserved. Their project was submitted not only to the Abbé Courtois and the Abbé Sauvé who already were well acquainted for years with Adèle's aspirations, but also to the Père Balme, of the Order of St Dominic, one of Lacordaire's first disciples, and himself a founder. This holy man, in spite of old age and many infirmities, was well known as a spiritual director of souls, and was the director of Alice. Adèle came to Paris in November to consult him about the work. On November 8, she and Alice made their communion at Our Lady of Victories, and consecrated themselves to God for His Church, through the hands of the Immaculate Mother. A little rule of life was also drawn up. This rule, written by Adèle, and corrected by Père Balme, is dated December 4. Its twelve chapters are terminated by the words which have become so dear to her Congregation: 'Amen! Alleluia!'

The year 1897 was destined to open with a cross, a great disappointment. The person on whom Adèle counted the most, withdrew from all participation in the work, and soon it became evident that she could not trust in the others. Adèle's whole life was one of abandonment to the divine Will, and she received this cross with her usual calm. But Alice had been far from well for some time, and how was she to be told? Would it not be too much for her to endure?

Père Balme himself told her of this blow. She wrote at once to her 'dearest mother in Jesus,' and told her that he seemed to be much afflicted by the news, but that he had been greatly edified by the calmness with which she had received it. The month of February passed in this peaceful waiting on God's Will, without any human hope of being able to begin the work; when suddenly, at the beginning of March, the clouds rolled away, the third sister was found, and they could begin to think seriously of the foundation. This was Alexida Bourgeois, to be known in the future as Mother Mary of St John, and to prove herself a worthy companion of Adèle and Alice, indeed (as I believe, for I knew her well), a Saint all but equal to the Mother to whom God gave her. Alexida was then eighteen, and came from Poitou. Very pious, very candid, she had a look in her eyes, which, as Adèle said, enabled you to read the very depths of her soul. She had, too, a heart of gold, capable of unlimited devotion to the cause.

Adèle met her first at St Varent, in October, 1896. Her idea at this time was to enter the Congregation of the Immaculate Conception at Lourdes. One day they happened to kneel side by side at the altar-rails to receive Holy Communion. Adèle felt at this moment an inner conviction that the girl kneeling beside her was destined one day to be her daughter in religion. But she said nothing about it at the time, as the vocation of the young girl seemed to be already decided.

During the stay that Adèle made at St Varent with her friend Mlle Vivon, Alexida never spoke to her at all intimately. It was only after she had left that the girl felt herself attracted to what Mlle Vivon used to call, 'the work of Mlle Garnier.' She asked eager questions about this work, and all she heard made her feel more and more that this was where God wanted her to be. She spoke of it to her director, who, to her surprise, entirely approved the idea. While this was going on, the defection of the lady chosen as Superior put a stop to the immediate carrying out of the work. As Père Balme said, 'It takes three monks to make a chapter.' Adèle wrote the sad news to Mlle Vivon, who replied:

'It is, indeed, a pity that you cannot begin, for Alexida would have been with you.' Adèle replied at once, 'But let her come and we will begin.'

It was then decided to begin the work in June, at Montmartre.

Adèle wrote to her second daughter a letter which defines very clearly the aspirations of the first Adorers of the Sacred Heart.

'PARIS, 14th March,

'MY VERY DEAR CHILD,

'I should have loved to tell you sooner the profound joy which I felt, and which I now share with your sister Alice, when M. l'Abbé was kind enough to tell me the good news of your union with us. A union at first of prayer and hopeful desire, and then as soon as the time fixed by your director has struck, a union which will become a reunion, a life in common, a life of fraternity and piety, an apprenticeship in fact to that life of holy religion, which is our vocation. You are drawn by an attraction (and after serious reflection, too, which shows the Will of God) to join yourself to two poor souls, who like yourself, have the unique desire better to serve Our Lord, and accomplish His Holy Will, by devoting themselves entirely and for ever to the Holy Church, to its visible Head, Our Holy Father the Pope, and to the clergy. To this end we devote ourselves with all our soul, while waiting to be devoted to it by the consecration of the Church, that is to work, pray and suffer, to immolate ourselves, if it please God, as poor and very unworthy little victims; victims, that is to say, offered to God the Father in union with Our Lord, the Divine Victim, offered by Him who is the Sovereign Priest.

'We say, then, "O my God, here we are, we are Thine, to do Thy Will. Deign to make us love it and fulfil it always in everything."

'In these dispositions we can, and ought, to expect trouble, difficulties, cares and trials of every kind, poverty, humiliation, perhaps even persecution. We must be prepared for sacrifice, always, always! For this, indeed, we must not only be prepared, but even eager, in obedience and with a deep humility and consciousness that we are nothing. We must realise that all that we may do and suffer and desire is absolutely nothing in itself, but, united to the merits of Our Lord, becomes of immense value in His eyes. Do you feel, my dear Alexida, that you are prepared thus to live?

'In a short time from now we will choose at Montmartre, and if it is possible, quite near the Basilica of the Sacred Heart, a little set of rooms sufficient for our needs, together with a spare room for our friends or sisters in the world, when they may desire to come and pass among us a few days of recollection and prayer. There at home, in this little dwelling which we shall love to call our Nazareth, thus putting ourselves under the protection of the Holy Family, we shall train ourselves little by little in the practice of the virtues proper to the religious state, under the guidance of a holy and experienced Religious Father, who has been good enough to assure us of his help. We shall see him, as a rule, once a week.

'You and Alice will be two little sisters, of whom I, on account of my age, will be the mother, and at the same time the sister and the servant in solicitude, affection and devotion. We shall have but one heart and one soul, and thus united we shall strive to sanctify ourselves in studying our divine Model, sustaining one another by advice, example and help; in a word, by charity always and in all things.

'Our life must be poor, through love and imitation of Our Lord, and in His poverty we shall bless the necessity which will oblige us to practise it, for, indeed, our resources will be very, very small. We shall have only what is absolutely necessary! Our Lord Himself never had more than that, indeed, He had not even that always. But He will deign to ask this for us and with us, when we recite the Paternoster. Oh, my sister, how happy shall we be in our sufferings if we truly love Jesus.

'We know nothing of the future, and we must not seek to know it. If Our Lord deigns to increase our little family, we shall bless Him, if He leaves us alone, we shall bless Him still, and we shall try to love Him even more if possible, to replace the Sisters whom we have not deserved to have.

'If it please God that our little work should begin to find its little realisation on the feast of St Peter and Paul, during the month of the Sacred Heart, it will be for us a very great consolation. But we wish to know no will but Our Lord's. All will be well! When you arrive we will go, your sister and I, to meet you, and bring you to our little convent, which will be ready, in its poverty, to receive you.

'If you are able to send me a few lines to tell me what you think of our plans, and whether you are pleased or frightened, please do so. But if you cannot do so easily, do not worry; your good director, or Mlle Vivon, will have the goodness to inform me of your state of mind.

'Together, then, we pray, now from afar, but later on united together, for God's Church, but also for our spiritual Fathers, for our families, for all our benefactors and their intentions. The wider the extent of our intercessions, the more will the Heart of Our Lord accept and bless them.

'Adieu, my very dear child, my daughter, my sister. May Our Lady of the Apostles protect you, may the Holy Angels watch over you, and may Our Lord pour out upon you ever His most precious blessings.

'Pray for your poor Mother.'

chapter eight

The First Beginnings At Montmartre

'IT was June 21, 1897,' Alice writes, 'that our Mother and I mounted the hill of Montmartre in order to take up our abode there. We had hired an apartment in a house number II bis, Rue du Mont Cenis. This house was named "The City of the Sacred Heart," and we called our own little dwelling in it "Nazareth," just as our Mother, twenty-one years before, had named the two poor attics in which she spent her first sojourn at Montmartre. We were so happy! With what ardour had we prayed at the feet of Jesus, exposed in the Blessed Sacrament in the Basilica. When we reached our dwelling, I remember that our Mother and I read together some pages of the Rule of St Benedict, to which we felt attracted.'

She goes on to describe Nazareth — a tiny set of rooms. There was a little room which for some months had to serve them for chapel, refectory, community room and parlour. There were two more, for sleeping, a tiny kitchen and that was about all. The furniture was very poor, and there was nothing which was not strictly necessary. They had bought one or two folding beds in case of future postulants. Indeed, a fourth sister joined them two days later. Alexida arrived on the day following the installation. They went to fetch her at the station. She was overflowing with joy, and flung herself into their arms. After a visit to Nazareth they went to the Basilica to thank the Sacred Heart. Next day the fourth sister arrived. She was a pious widow from a village of the Cote d'Or, who had been recommended by the Abbé Charles Sauvé; they called her Sister Teresa.

A little rule of life had been drawn up, and they followed it faithfully. They went to the Basilica for Mass, Adoration and Benediction. On June 24, which was the Vigil of the Feast of the Sacred Heart that year, they began to say Office together in their little oratory. It was at first the Office of Our Lady, but this was soon afterwards replaced by that of the Sacred Heart.

Thus in humility and poverty was the great work at last begun. On June 29 they descended into the crypt of the Basilica, and there consecrated themselves to St Peter, begging the Prince of the Apostles to adopt them as his children. They tried at first to keep their project secret from the Fathers who served the Basilica, until they had passed through a period of trial; but this did not last long. In the absence of Père Balme, their confessor, they went to confession to one of these Fathers, Père Vasseur, and had to confide to him their secret. He became their devoted friend and helper. But he kept their secret faithfully while it was necessary, for as Père Balme told them, they must remain for the time in the Catacombs. They received the Chains of St Peter from the Abbé Sauvé, who came to visit them, and wore them secretly beneath their clothing, as an emblem of their vocation.

Those first months were spent in an atmosphere of joy and thanksgiving; the crosses were to come later; but at present all was peace. They gave themselves seriously to the study of Latin, in order that they might enter more fully into the liturgical life of the Church. In September, Père Balme added to their joy by proposing that on November 21, Feast of the Presentation of Our Lady, he should clothe them with a little habit, and consecrate them in a very special manner to the Sacred Heart of Jesus. They might then begin a noviciate, not, indeed, a canonical noviciate, but one of preparation. This 'little habit' was a white scapular, having embroidered on it the Sacred Heart and the keys of St Peter, and on the other side a cross and the monogram of Mary. They were to wear it under their ordinary clothing.

This little ceremony took place at the Dominican Convent at Levallois-Perret, which had a hospital attached to it, where the aged Dominican Father was then residing. It was in the greatest secrecy, in his own little room in the hospital, that the clothing of the four future religious took place. The Father blessed the scapulars, and, placing them on their shoulders, gave to each the religious name which she had already chosen, adding to each name that of our Blessed Lady. They were all deeply moved, as was the Father himself. Then. he addressed them, in a voice trembling with emotion: 'You are still but a grain of mustard seed,' he said to them, 'but this little grain will shoot up and become a tree, a great tree under which many souls will come to take shelter.'

The six months which Père Balme desired that they should spend hidden and unknown, in order to prove their vocation and their perseverance, were now drawing to a close. And the sisters were every day more convinced that they were where Our Lord wanted them to be, more and more confirmed in their vocation. Adèle felt that it was now time to submit their project to the Superior of the Basilica, Fr John Baptist Lemius. They were not without anxiety, for they feared that he might very probably oppose their desire, or at any rate, at first. Père Vasseur, too, had his doubts, and hesitated to speak to him, even when he was begged to do so. However, a providential occasion soon arose, and Père Lemius became, for the little congregation, a true and devoted Father.

In January, 1898, Adèle was at prayer in the Basilica, when Our Lord deigned to communicate to her that St Michael had become Protector of the work. She was filled with joy and consolation at this new proof of the divine favour. Meanwhile, Père Lemius was occupying himself seriously with the work. He studied it closely, prayed for guidance and light, and soon found that it was time to lay the whole project before the Archbishop of Paris. He took with him letters from the Abbé Sauvé and the Abbé Courtois, containing their appreciations of Adèle and her work. The aged Père Balme was too ill to write. Père Lemius was received by the Cardinal, who, while he listened to him, seemed to be searching for a document that had gone astray. All at once he stopped looking for it. He sat down in his chair, an arm supporting his head. He shut his eyes and remained absorbed in profound thought, while the Father continued his story. From time to time he uttered slowly the word 'Yes!' When the Father had finished, the Cardinal looked at him earnestly and said, 'This is from God.'

It was, said Père Lemius, after his return home, as if the Cardinal had been listening to the recital of a work which he greatly desired. His Eminence proceeded to put the foundation in charge of his private secretary, M. l'Abbé Lefebvre. It was arranged that he should come to Montmartre on March 4, the first Friday of the month, and interview all the sisters. When he left the Cardinal's presence, Père Lemius had said to him: 'Eminence, you are the founder of this Community.' And the Cardinal replied, smiling: 'I won't say No.'

Père Lemius sent for Adèle and told her the happy news. When she returned to Nazareth her joyful face made her daughters at once comprehend that she was the bearer of good news. When they could hardly contain their impatience to hear her story, she said: 'My children, get ready the books, we are going to sing a Te Deum.'

A few days later the new Community received the official Act of Foundation, ratified by the Cardinal, dated March 4, 1898, and the novitiate began on that day. The Sacred Heart had thus at last answered and rewarded the long expectation of Adèle Garnier. The religious Congregation which she had seen in spirit so many years before was now founded on the holy mountain. But what in her profound humility she had not foreseen was, that it was she herself who was to offer to Our Lord this religious family born in the wound of the divine Heart. There was now question of drawing up Constitutions or a set of rules for the Congregation. These were discussed by Père

Lemius and Père Balme, together with the Mother Foundress, as we may now name Adèle. She chose for the device of the Congregation, *Gloria Deo per Sacratissimum Cor Jesu,* and this has become permanent.

And now the crosses that she had foreseen began to present themselves. A new subject had joined them, after they had been at Nazareth about seven months, and as she was very capable as well as very devout, she was named Mistress of Novices. But the whole Community, including the Foundress and herself, were but novices, and it soon became evident that a mistake had been made. The new-comer never really shared the spirit of the Congregation, and probably never really had a religious vocation at all. But Adèle's humility made her fancy herself entirely unfit to govern a Community, and she hoped that she would be able to hand over the reins to the new-comer, and retire herself into the state of submission for which she always craved. When it became clear that the new Mistress of Novices was not in her right place, the Mother had too deep a sense of responsibility for the children God had given her to remain passive. She prayed more earnestly than ever, she sought for an indication of the divine Will, and each morning at Holy Communion an inner voice told her, 'She will not remain.'

At last she was obliged to consult Père Lemius, and it was decided that the Ecclesiastical Superior must intervene. After his visit, the Mistress of Novices herself decided to depart. She left on June 9, in peace and cordiality. At the end of April, 1898, the little Community took a larger set of rooms, still, however, in the same house. They were then able to reserve a room to be their oratory. In the same month, a Benedictine monk, Dom Remi Buzy, came to give them conferences. He was from the first a true and devoted friend.

New postulants presented themselves, so that on July 2, 1899, the Sisters were able to begin Perpetual Adoration of the Blessed Sacrament during the day. On Christmas Eve the first lay-sister postulant entered the Community. She was a little

Breton, named Marie Noelle. She had been a shepherdess, and used to recite her rosary while watching over her sheep; sometimes she would say even twenty chaplets a day. Then she came to Paris as a servant, and here she heard of the new foundation and conceived a most earnest desire to join it. She could neither read nor write. Unhappily she was able to remain at Montmartre only a few months. She was not strong, and was threatened with consumption. However, she was received into another Community in her own land, where the Sisters occupied themselves with work in the fields. And here she was able to make profession. But as her short stay at Montmartre led to the institution of lay-sisters in the Community, her memory remains dear to her former sisters in religion.

The year 1899 was to be one of the first importance to our little Community. It was to witness the reception of the habit by the first postulants, and the religious profession of Adèle Garnier and her companions. It was surely no coincidence that it was also to be marked by the solemn consecration of the whole human race to the Sacred Heart of Jesus, made by the Holy Father himself.

The first night of adoration began on March 15, and it was decided that it should be repeated on the first Friday of every month. The Sisters had not yet the happiness of possessing the Blessed Sacrament in their poor little home, but they arose hour by hour in turn, to adore Jesus in the silence of their cells, and the adoration was directed to Him in His Eucharistic glory in the Basilica. On March 17 two Sisters received the habit as novices. (The four elders had become novices without any ceremony.) This first ceremonial clothing was presided over by M. Lefebvre, assisted by Père Lemius. There were present beside the Mother and five Sisters in the choir, Père Vasseur, who had been their first friend at the Basilica, and one who was to be a great benefactor of the Community, Mme Legentil.

The Cardinal desired that the profession of Adèle and her first children should take place on the Feast of the Sacred

Heart. This fell that year on June 9. The Encyclical of Leo XIII, announcing the consecration of the whole human race to the Sacred Heart, had recently been published, and we can imagine with what joy and thanksgiving this had filled the hearts of Adèle and her daughters. The profession was preceded by a retreat, which passed in the most profound peace, and their hearts were filled with joy and happiness. The evening before the profession, Adèle, kneeling before her daughters, asked their pardon for everything in which she had failed with regard to them. They could not contain their tears, and they embraced one another weeping.

The ceremony of profession took place, by special privilege, in the crypt of the Basilica, in the Chapel of St Peter, which is immediately under the High Altar. Canon Lefebvre presided at the function, as Ecclesiastical Superior, and was assisted by Père Lemius.

Several centuries before this, St Ignatius Loyola and his first companions had made their profession on the same holy hill, in the crypt of the chapel which commemorates the martyrdom of St Denis. And here, in the crypt of a sanctuary still more august, were laid, at this new profession, the spiritual foundations of Adèle's work for the Sacred Heart. Two days later, on Sunday, June 11, took place the consecration of the human race to this Adorable Heart. This consecration, Adèle decided, should be recited every day by her daughters in choir, and this has become one of the most cherished traditions of her religious family.

chapter nine

A Benedictine Vocation

A LITTLE after the profession, the Community began to practise regularly the Adoration of the Blessed Sacrament during the day, which had always been their aim and desire. They began in July, 1899, and even then their numbers made it sometimes very difficult, supposing that one of them were ill, or otherwise prevented. But they persevered none the less. They had to go out to the Basilica for this, whatever the weather. But from this date there was, all the day long, at least one Sister kneeling before Our Lord exposed in the Monstrance from five-thirty in the morning to eight o'clock in the evening. Each adoration lasted at least one hour. At this time they were only nine in number, so it is clear that the practice must have entailed great sacrifices.

It became more than ever desirable for them to establish themselves in the new abode, which divine Providence had seemed to point out to them, as soon as that were possible. There they would have a chapel with the Blessed Sacrament and there they could make their adoration without going outside.

The house they had decided on was No. 40 Rue de la Barre, near to the Basilica of the Sacred Heart. It was quite a large property, with a wooded park, and several cottages. The purchase of this property had an interesting introduction. Père Lemius was saying Mass at the well-known Sanctuary of Notre Dame de la Garde at Marseilles. All at once, at the offertory of the Mass (as he tells us himself), he had a distraction quite unaccountable at the time. The words '40 Rue de la Barre, the Sisters' Convent,' entered into his mind with such force and such importunity that he could not drive them away. It so seized on his imagination, that he whispered to Our Lady: 'Why should you not give them this place, so suitable for your dear Community?' What was not his astonishment when, on returning to Paris, a house-agent presented himself and offered him this very property for sale! The price asked at first was no less than 800,000 francs. However, after discussion, this was reduced to 500,000. Even this sum seemed absolutely impossible for a Community so poor.

The owner soon announced that he was willing to take 150,000 at first, and that the rest might be paid in course of time to be arranged between him and the purchasers. The owner was anxious, if possible, to sell it to the religious for the work of the Sacred Heart. He would give them the preference over other bidders, and would let them have it at a more modest price. It was finally agreed on, and the contract was signed on May 19, 1899.

In the month of November a payment of 50,000 francs towards the acquisition of the new property had to be made. They had counted on receiving this from a source which failed them. They betook themselves to prayer, and presently Père Lemius arrived with a paper in his hand. It was exactly the sum required! It had been given him by a lady who took a great interest in the new foundation. She became the first 'Foundress' of the new Convent.

More help came from the Carthusian Fathers of the Grande Chartreuse. Before their cruel expulsion they used to spend the greater part of their revenues in good works. Cardinal Richard encouraged Père Lemius to put the case before the Fathers, and promised to write to them himself. The Prior of the Grande Chartreuse replied to Père Lemius saying, that if possible he would like him to come there, so that they might discuss together the amount which should be given. And in a few days the zealous Father was there. To his great joy, the Carthusian Prior told him that they had agreed to devote to the work the large sum of a 100,000 francs (which in those days was equivalent to £4000). They had been specially moved by the promise that in return for this charity the Sisters would perpetually plead for the Carthusian Order before the throne of the divine Heart. The money was duly paid in instalments during the following year. And ever since the Adorers of the Sacred Heart have been intimately linked by spiritual bonds with the great Order of St Bruno.

Meanwhile, the good Dominican who had done for them such wonderful things lay on his death-bed. He sent, by means of one of his brethren, his tender adieux to Adèle and her little family. He begged them ever to remember him before the Adorable Heart to whose adoration they were pledged. Father Balme lived yet some weeks, and died on February 25, 1900, about midnight. It would seem that almost all the great religious Orders had their part in the foundation of Adèle's work. We have already seen what the Jesuits had done for her, the Dominicans in the person of Père Balme had aided in their turn, and now the Carthusians had come to her assistance. And as we shall see, the oldest of our religious Orders, that of St Benedict, was one day to crown the whole work.

Adèle, even at this early time, was filled with desire to number her little flock among the children of St Benedict. That desire was indeed destined to be fully satisfied, but its complete accomplishment was as yet a matter for the future. Yet, even now, she desired to unite her Congregation to the great Order of the monastic patriarch.

For some time they had been increasingly struck by the harmony which existed between the Benedictine spirituality and their own vocation. The thought that if they had this Rule for their guide they would perhaps obtain deliverance from their present suffering, or at least more grace and strength to support it, had struck the Mother very forcibly, as she wrote to Père Lemius a few days later. They had drawn up a report on this subject with a view to presenting it to their ecclesiastical superiors. They did not ask to become Benedictines, in the strict sense of the word, but that while remaining what they were, with their own aim of life, their constitutions and special devotions, they might adopt the Rule of St Benedict, as the 'type of religious life and foundation of perfection,' while joining to its practice the modifications and additions required by the special needs and aim of their Congregation.

The Divine Office: the prescription of the Rule 'that nothing be preferred to the Work of God' (i.e. that that must dominate all their occupations) was their very *raison d'être*. For them it included not only the recitation of the Breviary in common, but also the perpetual adoration. *Silence* again, insisted on so strongly in that Holy Rule, was also with them one of the observances most strictly prescribed. Another of the principal foundations of the Rule was continual work, both intellectual and manual. And this was also their own aim, from the very beginning. *Penance,* an essential obligation of Christianity, and one which was so forcibly inculcated by St Benedict, was their very life, since they were consecrated to a life of reparation and immolation. Again, *Works of Zeal,* as practised among them, were absolutely in accordance with the spirit of this holy Rule. Their great work was prayer, they were contemplatives, but this by no means excluded their working for souls, any more than it did in Benedictine monasteries. The observance of the Rule would, in fact, help them to give to such works the character of religion and discretion, and guarantee them in the future from taking up works which might tend to the detriment of their life of prayer. As to interior observances, those which characterise the Benedictine Rule, were just those which were observed the most strenuously among themselves. This holy Rule would give them a new authority, and better ensure their continuance.

Obedience, for instance, is the fundamental virtue of the Rule. The holy legislator explains in detail its practice, its qualities and degrees. To make a religious society strong and stable, no better foundation could be found. *Humility* is the keynote of the Rule; St Benedict enlarges on this virtue with more detail than on any other. Not only does the admirable chapter on the twelve degrees of Humility form the most striking part of the Rule, but every page is full of it. And the Mother felt that its teaching was most admirably adapted to the needs of the little society, consecrated, as it was, to 'Jesus meek and humble of heart.' *The Spirit of Prayer* prescribed by the Rule must also inspire the lives of those who were called to Adoration in spirit and in truth; to continual prayer for the Church, for the clergy, for the conversion of sinners, always by and through the Sacred Heart of Jesus. *The Spirit of Sacrifice and Penance* inspires each page of the Rule, and that, too, must be particularly their own.

Such, Adèle felt, was exactly what should be the spirit of a religious vowed to reparation, reparation which embraced not only expiation for their own sins, but reparation for the outrages offered to the Heart of Jesus in the Holy Eucharist, and for the sins of France. *The Family Spirit* is especially a keynote of the Benedictine Rule; and that, too, is the spirit which she most wished to cultivate among her daughters. It includes affection, humble, submissive, filial, towards superiors; a charity cordial, devoted, simple, but full of respect and reverence one for the other; and that is what she strove to practise and to teach. Lastly, *Discretion,* a very prominent feature of St Benedict's teaching, was a virtue which she most earnestly desired to see practised among them, lest by over-zeal the duties of their observance should be allowed to injure their health. By this, too, they would learn to help one another, to serve one another to the greater glory of the Sacred Heart.

It was on March 9, 1901, a few days after the Cardinal's visit, that Adèle took this report to M. Lefebvre and begged him to submit it to His Eminence; she also told him of their ardent desire to have the Blessed Sacrament reserved among them, as soon as they were settled in their new abode. On the 19th, the Feast of St Joseph, they had the joyful news that the Cardinal fully approved, and that he granted both their petitions. They were to follow the Rule of St Benedict, and they were to have the Blessed Sacrament reserved in their new abode.

chapter ten

The New Abode - the Assaults Of Satan

ON May 24, 1901, Adèle and her daughters took possession of the new property. It was the Feast of Our Lady, Help of Christians, and they were indeed to need her help.

They occupied two cottages standing near one another, and united by their garden. One they called St Benedict's and the other St Bruno's. Friends had come to their help in a wonderful way, but the installation had been long delayed by various difficulties. And now the political outlook in France was becoming very dark, as M. Combes and his Government were threatening new laws of persecution against the Church and more especially against the Religious Orders.

A large room in the upper story of one of the cottages became the chapel. Dom Remy came on the 29th to give them instructions in the Benedictine Rule, and on the 31st Père Lemius blessed the new Convent. The first Mass was said there on June 1, by the same Father, and on the night of June 6-7 they made their first night of adoration before the Blessed Sacrament exposed on the altar of their chapel. In this same year they entered into close relations with Solesmes. Their charter of affiliation to the great Abbey founded by Dom Guéranger is dated July 2, 1901. The Solesmes nuns of the monastery of Ste Cécile were kind enough to give them a copy of their Constitutions, drawn up by Dom Guéranger, in the form of Declarations on the Benedictine Rule, and these were of the greatest possible use to them in drawing up their own Constitutions and in helping them to become true daughters of St Benedict.

It is now necessary to enter upon a matter of some difficulty. The Sisters, even before leaving their little Nazareth, had had some experience of a great trial which became now more intense and more terrible. Those who know the history of the beginnings of various religious Orders, and more especially of those of the Order of St Benedict, will not be surprised to learn that the devil seems to have employed his most furious machinations against this infant community which was devoted to prayer for the Church of God.

We shall here follow strictly, in the account of what happened, the narration drawn up by the Co-Foundress of the Institute, Alice Andrade, now known as Mother Agnes of the Sacred Heart. Those who knew her intimately, as the present writer had the happiness to do, well know that every word she says comes from a soul, not only closely united to Our Lord, but also gifted with exceptional powers of intelligence and common sense. We have also heard from Adèle herself a sufficient description of these cruel trials to leave no doubt as to their absolute accuracy. On the other hand, the writer has had conversations on the subject with an old friend of the Community, a Canon of the Cathedral of Sens, which tended to throw some doubt, not indeed on the phenomena, but on the source of some at least of them. It is quite possible that some of them, he said, may have been due, not directly to diabolical interposition, but to the trickery and bad faith of one of the novices, who afterwards had to leave the Community, and who confessed to him enough to make him believe this. But when the writer talked this over later with Mother Agnes, she told him of phenomena which could not apparently have possibly been due to any human agent.

We will now follow the account the same Mother has left us.

'The trial presented two principal characteristics. There were facts of the material order. There were also cases of obsession and diabolical possession, even, it would seem, of "exterior possession," to quote Père De Haze, S.J., one of the exorcists appointed by Cardinal Richard. These cases constituted the most cruel part of the trial; first because they were directed against some of our own Sisters, and also because of the frightful noises and appalling manifestations that accompanied them. In December, 1900, two novices and a postulant were directly attacked. One was a good little lay-sister, who seems to have received from Our Lord quite special graces. The postulant, who had many good qualities, seemed to me never to have had a real religious vocation, but of that we could not then be sure. In the case of the second novice, I should rather be inclined to see a case of obsession, favoured by a weak constitution.

'I know how natural it would be, for those who were not witnesses of what happened, to ascribe the whole thing to psychopathic trouble in these cases; and indeed I am quite disposed to think that such natural causes may well have produced certain of the phenomena, or at any rate contributed to them. On the other hand, I am bound in truth to declare, that if I consider the trial as a whole, I cannot see how it can possibly be explained in a convincing manner if one excludes (taking the whole of the facts into consideration) the hypothesis of diabolical intervention. With the exception of our Superiors and the Fathers concerned, we naturally tried to keep the whole matter as secret as possible. It was a terrible tribulation which weighed on us, but divine Providence came to our aid in a marvellous manner. ... In April, 1901, there appeared several times fragments of the bread used to make hosts. Wherever they may have come from, the mode of their appearance seems to me to be incapable of a natural explanation. The particles appeared suddenly without any visible exterior agency. One day they appeared in the Refectory during dinner, in the sight of the whole Community. (They looked exactly like the small hosts received at Holy Communion, they seemed to fall from the ceiling.) They were on the table, on the ground, on our clothes. One day, they made their appearance in the presence of

Canon Penportier, the Promotor of the Faith. M. Lefebvre had several of the particles submitted to a chemical analysis, and it was proved that they were in fact made of the unleavened bread used for hosts.

'One of our Sisters, persecuted by the demon, used to receive ringing blows on the face from him. We could hear these blows resound, but could not see the hand that gave them. ... Our Mother Foundress and I had our rooms on the ground-floor of St Bruno's; one morning a little after we had installed ourselves there, our Mother had gone out and I was making the Adoration. A Sister who was returning from the Basilica heard in our rooms a horrible noise which lasted some seconds. She knocked at the doors, but hearing no answer went to Mère Marie de St Jean. The two Sisters tried to enter the rooms, but found they were locked, which was quite contrary to our custom. Guessing that this was one of the demon's tricks, Mère St Jean took a key, the first she came across. The door opened; in fact they could enter both rooms. The most extraordinary spectacle presented itself. In the two cells, everything they contained—tables, chairs, stools, pictures, crucifixes, papers, books, washing-stands, crockery—all had been thrown on the ground in heaps in a disorder impossible to describe. But there was nothing broken.

'Meanwhile, the Mother and I had returned. What struck us most was that a basin full of water had been overturned, but not a drop of water had escaped; there were also open ink-stands flung on the floor, but not a drop of the ink had been spilt, which, naturally speaking, was quite impossible. The keys were found on the floor, one hidden under the bed-clothes, another was in a box, thrown down in the middle of the room. Another room, that occupied by our benefactress, Madame Auban Moet, who used it from time to time to make a retreat in our little monastery, had also been invaded. We heard a wild dance going on in this room. When we entered it, we found everything overturned. A plaster statuette of the Sacred Heart was lying on the floor, but this, though so fragile, was absolutely intact. Soon afterwards a similar fracas began elsewhere. Here the furniture had all been flung in the direction of the door. Two tables had been thrown over, but the table-cloths were still in place. The ink-stand had been flung on the ground upside down, but here too not a drop of ink was spilt.

'What has remained fixed in my memory was a wild dance made by various objects on the staircase. Our Mother wrote of this: "I had not yet gone to bed, when a new noise, ringing through the house, an *insolent* noise, was heard on the staircase. I looked out and saw plates and cups and saucers violently rolling about, clashing against each other, with a horrible noise, I looked higher up the staircase, and found that it was absolutely covered with them. ... I went down again, and was not yet in bed, when I heard an infernal noise of iron and crockery. I ran to the staircase, and I saw a pair of enormous tongs dancing down the staircase, with huge bounds; there was also a shovel which the demon had found in the attic, and which he had flung down upon the crockery with fury, breaking it into pieces." '

Mother Agnes continues: 'Hearing this hullabaloo I opened my door, which was close to the staircase, and I still recall my stupefaction on seeing these heavy tongs which descended the stairs, just as if they were alive, making the most extravagant bounds. I could mention other extraordinary happenings, as, for instance, the clothes of one of the victims being suddenly all whisked off, in the twinkling of an eye, in presence of the other Sisters. These clothes disappeared and were only brought back three or four days later, at the command of the exorcist. But I think that there is no need to enlarge any further on this matter. What I cannot omit, however, what, indeed, it is sweet to remember, is the admirable patience, the peace, the serenity of our beloved Mother Foundress. She had that confidence in God which nothing could ever disturb, and which was most splendidly rewarded by Him; for a trial such as this, occurring as it did in the capital of France, seemed, humanly speaking, bound to bring about the destruction of this little Community which was as yet scarcely founded.'

By the month of August these distressing attacks had ceased. During their continuance, the Community had been greatly consoled and strengthened by the help given to them by their Superiors. But they felt it was Our Lady herself who had intervened once more to chain the demon. And the Feast of her Assumption was celebrated with a special joy and splendour.

But if the powers of hell were chained, they had not ceased to work in other and more dangerous ways. Another cruel persecution was preparing, one that would drive them from the Holy Mountain whither God had called their Mother in so marvellous a manner; they were to be driven out, not merely from Montmartre, but from their dear country, to whose salvation they were devoted, and sent into another land which knew them not. At the beginning of July, 1901, the infamous law of the 'Associations' had been promulgated, which ordered the dissolution of every religious Community not authorised by the Government, or which had not solicited this authorisation within a period of three months. Every institution asking for such authorisation had to submit to the examination of the Government, its rule and statutes, and also its temporal possessions, income and resources. It had thus to expose itself to the confiscation of everything it possessed.

By the end of August there remained no more hope of any mitigation of these conditions. What was our little Community to do? After long examination, and many prayers, they decided that, whatever happened, they must not separate from one another, but must continue the common life, which was so dear to them. If it could not be at Montmartre, they must go into exile. They dared not ask the authorisation of the Government, for they knew what that entailed. The Mother submitted the matter to the Cardinal. At first he thought that if they remained quietly at Montmartre, they had more to hope for than to fear. They were immensely relieved at this decision.

But only a few days later, the Cardinal, afraid lest he should have incurred too heavy a responsibility by his advice to remain, asked them to consult a well-known Catholic lawyer, as to the risks they would run as regards their property. He examined the whole situation with the greatest possible exactitude, and decided that it was impossible for them to remain. They could not hope to pass as an ordinary Association, there were too evident signs of their being a religious community. If they did not ask for authorisation, they would be dissolved *ipso facto*. If, on the other hand, they did ask for it, he was assured that it would not be granted, and in this case they would have to depart all the same, and their property would be confiscated by the government. This would be to compromise other interests than their own, for a part of the price paid for the property had been borrowed from their friends.

In these conditions the path of duty seemed clear; and the Cardinal fully approved their determination to leave, much as he grieved at their departure. A friend of the Community had suggested that if they could not live together, they might separate for a time, and live two and two in lodgings on the hill, and thus continue the adoration. But the Mother saw that that would be quite impossible. 'In three months,' she wrote, 'we should have undone the work of four years, and there is not one of our Sisters who would not prefer exile to this, even if it had to be endured for years. As to myself, who feel my heart torn in pieces at the idea of quitting Montmartre, yet I trust not to lack the courage nor swerve from the responsibility to lead them to a foreign land. ... But to remain here under the conditions proposed would be to sacrifice the religious life to the consolation of not leaving Montmartre.'

They all agreed in this. They were willing to go far away in spite of their poverty, trusting in the Sacred Heart to come to their aid, as in times past.

Adèle wrote to Père Lemius: 'Father, the Sacred Heart is there! He will feed us, He will not allow us to want the necessities of life. He knows that it is Himself who is our leader and guide, and He will watch over us there, as He has done here. When the Apostles quitted the Cœnaculum, their sorrow was great. They had to leave that dear spot, where they had lived with Our Lord, where they had seen Him die. They were not rich, they had no sure means of subsistence; but their good Master had said: "Seek ye first the Kingdom of God and His justice, and all the rest shall be added unto you." Father, I know it, I feel it, I believe it firmly: this trial will turn to the glory of the Sacred Heart, to our sanctification, and to the development of our little Congregation.'

Brave words these, and worthy of her who wrote them, at the most painful crisis of her life. She remembered, doubtless, what Our Lord had said to her, at the end of her first sojourn at Montmartre, when she felt herself at the point of death. 'I have not led thee here that thou shouldest take root here, that will be only in Heaven. Follow the path before thee, as Abraham did, until I have shown to thee the place of the last Sacrifice.' That place was soon, indeed, to be shown her, though as yet she knew it not; it was to be Tyburn!

The approbation of the Cardinal had brought peace and consolation to the Mother, for here, as in all the changing scenes of her life, she sought nothing but the manifestation of the divine Will. But where were they to go? They turned their eyes towards England, that Protestant land, which was yet receiving with such extraordinary kindness and charity the Religious Communities exiled from France. They had no hesitation as to this, it must be England, and if possible, London. The Mother had experienced already, as have so many saints, a great drawing to prayer for the conversion of England; she felt an inward presentiment that her Congregation was called to take its part in this great work: she had known for some time that one day they would have a house of prayer in London.

She herself and Mother Agnes, her first companion, both knew the English language, in fact, the latter (Alice Andrade) had, as will be remembered, an English mother. They knew that they were sure of every possible help and kindness from Cardinal Vaughan, the devoted Archbishop of Westminster, and already they looked forward to establishing a house of prayer for the needs of their adopted country. They little knew then that they were destined to occupy the most sacred spot in all that land, the site of the death and the witness of at least a hundred martyrs for the Catholic Faith. Tyburn, the Calvary of England, was, indeed, another and a more sacred Montmartre. For Montmartre means 'the mount of Martyrs,' and is the reputed site of the martyrdom of St Denis.

Cardinal Richard had himself, it may be added, a special devotion to prayer for the Conversion of our country, and in 1897, the very year of the establishment of Adèle and her daughters at Montmartre, had ordered that a Mass should be said on the first Monday of every month at Notre Dame des Victoires for the return of England to the faith of her fathers. After Mass, the prayer of Leo XIII, so familiar to us all, was to be recited for this intention: 'Look down in mercy on England, thy Dowry.' On September 8, the Feast of the Nativity of Our Lady, he formally authorised the transfer of the Community to the diocese of Westminster.

And thus, after the assaults of Satan had been vanquished, his new machinations against this and the other religious Communities of France, were destined to help most powerfully in bringing back the dowry of Mary to its ancient Faith and allegiance.

chapter eleven

The Departure From Montmartre

BEFORE leaving France, Adèle and her three first daughters had the joy of being able to make their perpetual vows of religion. Up to now they had renewed them each year. The ceremony took place on September 27. But before this final oblation took place, the Mother, with her first companion, Alice Andrade (now Mother Agnes of the Sacred Heart), paid a flying visit to England, in order to place their plans before Cardinal Vaughan, and to find a shelter for the Community. They left Montmartre on September 13, the anniversary of the day when Adèle had had to leave it five-and-twenty years before, when, after her months of solitude there, she was taken away in what was thought to be a dying condition.

On reaching London, they took refuge at St Edward's Convent of Mercy in Harewood Avenue, where they were most kindly received. Two Canons of Paris were going to England the day after they left, and Cardinal Richard had arranged with them to prepare Cardinal Vaughan for their visit. But unfortunately he was absent from home, and this led to unexpected difficulties. However, they were received most kindly by his auxiliary, Bishop Brindle, on September 20. He was good enough at once to assure them of his paternal interest in the poor exiles, and to promise them that when they found a suitable dwelling, they would have permission for all they needed, a chapel with the Blessed Sacrament, open to the public for adoration.

They fixed, eventually, on a house in Notting Hill, 4 Bassett Road. It was not far from St Charles' College, and they knew that in case of need they could count on the ministrations of the Oblate Fathers of St Charles. Everywhere they were received with the greatest possible kindness and sympathy. The Mother wrote to Père Lemius, that in spite of the mountain of difficulties that faced them, there was something unspeakably consoling which dominated the whole situation.

'It is the presence of Our Lord which is to me just now as sensible as it was during the first year at Montmartre. I feel myself carried along, and accompanied by Him wherever I go. Nothing alarms me, though I have no idea as to what we are going to do. We live from day to day; tired out in the evening, so much as to think that we shall be unable to move the next day; and yet we begin again without the least trouble. God is, indeed, with us. And everywhere we are received with the most touching sympathy. Sometimes we are moved to tears by it, and absolutely surprised.'

After all had been settled, they returned to France, on September 25. They found the Sisters full of fervour, and already prepared for the departure. Adèle's sister, Joséphine, volunteered to come with them, and help to install them in their new home. They were touched and deeply moved here, too, by the sympathy shown them by their neighbours and friends. All kinds of people, even the poorest, vied with one another in sending them offerings. When they went out they were surrounded; people, often in tears, would cry out: 'Is it possible that you can be leaving us?' Adèle, indeed, had gained all hearts by her kindness and amiability. As Cardinal Mercier said of her, later: 'This woman is altogether lost in God, and she gives herself to her neighbour with the most marvellous simplicity.'

Père Lemius had already removed the Blessed Sacrament from the chapel, and all that was possible had already been packed up for the journey. On the 27th, then, on the very eve of their definite departure, the foundress and her three daughters made their perpetual Profession; and at the same time, two novices made their simple vows. The ceremony took place at six-thirty in the Basilica, at the altar of St Peter in the crypt. Canon Lefebvre presided, and he preached to his little flock on the Flight into Egypt. Père Lemius and Père Vasseur were present. This solemn ceremony definitely sealed the union of Adèle and her first children to the Sacred Heart of Jesus.

The house in Bassett Road not yet being ready for their occupation, it was arranged that the Sisters should, with Cardinal Richard's approbation, go and stay for a week or two with their relations or friends. The Fathers, too, were quitting Montmartre; it was a complete separation. M. Charles Michel, the devoted friend of the community, was good enough to take over the lease of the Convent at Montmartre, in order to watch over it, in the hope of their return.

To Adèle this parting was especially painful. All their hopes, all her prayers were centred round Montmartre, the departure was a trial far more bitter than death. Yet she endured with a heroic constancy, a complete submission to the divine Will, which reveals, indeed, how far she had advanced in sanctity. She wrote to Père Lemius: 'Ah! this Heart adorable and adored; indeed, He knows how to make tribulation and suffering loved by the hearts He has chosen for Himself. And how is it possible not to rejoice in the most agonising trials, when we know, when we feel that they form "the better part" chosen by His love: when we know that there is no more fruitful means of making His faithful participate in the work of saving souls, in the work of expiation! May He be loved, blessed and thanked, always and everywhere!'

The Mother and some of her daughters went to stay at Villeneuve-sur-Yonne with Mlle Joséphine Garnier. The departure for England was made in three groups. They were only eleven in all, seven professed Sisters, two Novices and two Postulants. On October 9, Mother Agnes took the first group across the channel. She, it will be remembered, was herself half English. Next day, Mother St John (Alexida) took the second group. The Mother had come to Paris to see them off. On that same day she went to take leave of their Superior, Canon Lefebvre, who was much grieved at the departure. But he said: 'It is a happy thing that you have decided to leave France, for the way things are going, you would have very soon seen the Community dissolved and the property confiscated.'

She saw, too, the General of the Oblates of Mary Immaculate, who, up to now, had served the Basilica. He told her that he had recommended them very specially to the Fathers of the Congregation at Kilburn. She then returned to spend a few more days at Villeneuve, and here Dom Remy came to see her. The night before, as she wrote to Père Lemius, she had taken leave of the dear Basilica. She went there to make a last Adoration. 'Oh, how great is this sacrifice. ... But I think of heaven—I think of the work and of the suffering which is absolutely necessary for us. That night I felt this call, always more forcible, more pressing, to a total renunciation, to a complete abnegation, to the acceptance, loving, eager, without regret or bitterness, of all possible sacrifices, all for the glory and consolation of His divine Heart. Yes, it is that, absolutely that, that He asks of us. And it is necessary that our daughters understand it, desire it, experience it, and that it enters into the souls, the blood, into the life and the actions of those that come after them. ... They must know that they themselves count for nothing; and that if they wish to work perseveringly and seriously for the sanctification of their souls, they must sacrifice themselves in everything and always for the glory of God, immolate themselves absolutely for the Sacred Heart, in order to win souls for Him. For our dear France, so guilty, but above all so deeply to be pitied; for England, whither the Sacred Heart calls us; for the Church, the beloved bride of Christ; for His Vicar, our beloved Father. For the honour and worship of Mary Immaculate, for the love and devotion towards the saints whom Jesus loves so tenderly, and whom He has given to us to honour and to imitate. ...

'Dear Father, we pray for you, pray for us, in order that we may all live only for Christ, and that with Him we may ever be able to say, "My meat is to do the will of my Father." You will tell them, too, that in every good work, if they desire to succeed for God's glory, they must for themselves desire humiliations, failures and disappointments.'

It was on October 14 that Adèle made her last adoration at Montmartre, and it was on the 15th, the feast of the great foundress, St Theresa, she came to England with the last group of her Sisters. Mother Agnes writes: 'I remember that when we disembarked at Folkestone, I wanted to kiss the soil of this dear and hospitable land, where we were going to be permitted to practise our monastic life in full liberty, according to the vocation to which the divine Heart of Jesus had called us. It was also the flame of the apostolate which enkindled our souls, under the action of the charity of Christ. We loved to remember St Augustine and the Benedictine monks who accompanied him, coming to this England to bring it the grace of the Catholic Faith. And we ourselves, little as we were, but supporting our littleness on the Heart of Jesus, we, too, were coming to labour, within the limits of our vocation, in the great work of the conversion of England... "On the mission, not in exile," such was the spirit that inspired us then.'

chapter twelve

Tyburn

W HAT could a little band of exiles, but lately formed, unknown and insignificant, do for the land which had given them shelter? Mother Agnes has told us that they came as missioners, not as exiles. They were to spend seventeen months in the little house in Bassett Road. They began to live there in Community on October 12, 1901. From the beginning they received from all sides the most touching marks of sympathy and charity. The first Office they recited there was the first Vespers of the Feast of St Edward the Confessor. But the last detachment of the little Community did not arrive till the feast of the great foundress, St Teresa, October 15. They had only a little room wherein to say their Offices, for the chapel was not ready until some weeks later.

On November 21, the Feast of Our Lady's Presentation (the *Dies Memorabilis* of the English Benedictine Congregation), they were clothed for the first time in their religious habit. (They had not been able to wear this at Montmartre.) It was a white habit, with blue girdle, red scapular, and a white choir cloak.[1] Four years earlier, on the same feast, the first Mothers had received the 'little habit,' or scapular, from Père Balme, O.P.

They had to go out to Mass, to the Church of the Sacred Heart at Kilburn which is in charge of the same Congregation of the Oblates of Mary Immaculate, who had until now served the Basilica of Montmartre. Clothed, then, in their new habits, they made pilgrimage thither, and their good Father Lemius,

---

[1] The habits had been made, under the Mother's superintendence, at the Frécault house at Villeneuve-sur-Yonne.

who had come to England in order to do all that lay in his power to help them, offered the Holy Sacrifice for their intentions. The Rector of the Church, Father James O'Reilly, received them with the greatest possible kindness, and remained their devoted friend until his death.

On December 6, the first Friday of the month, they had the joy and consolation of receiving Jesus among them once more. Père Lemius offered Mass in their little chapel, and the Community bound themselves by vow to represent England before the Sacred Heart of Jesus, and to offer their adorations and prayers night and day in a special manner for our country and for the return to Holy Church of its separated children.

Cardinal Vaughan had given his approval to the formula of this vow, which was, indeed, the expression of his own most ardent desires.[1] The Mother was inspired by the National Vow which was, as we have seen, the origin of the Basilica at Montmartre, and the inspiration of her own vocation. She was to lay down in the Constitutions of her Congregation, that each Convent would have a special mission of prayer and reparation on behalf of the country in which it was established. And here, in England, the nucleus of the future Congregation was to be devoted to the conversion of this country.

This humble community of French exiles, hidden away in their little house in Notting Hill, was to be set on a candlestick, to be charged with the mission of fulfilling a prediction[2] made more than three hundred years before, of raising a sanctuary of continual prayer, adoration and reparation at the spot where the Martyrs suffered. For this Community was to be stationed at Tyburn, the one spot in England most appropriate to the mission to which the Sacred Heart had called them.

---

[1] The text will be found in the Appendix. It is solemnly repeated every year on the Feast of the Epiphany.

[2] It was predicted by one of our confessors for the Faith that some future day a religious house would be established on this sacred spot. This prophecy, made by Father Gregory Gunne, was now at last to be fulfilled.

And here the present writer can speak with more authority, for it was in the early days at Tyburn that he first knew and began with the Mother who is the subject of this memoir, a friendship—one of the greatest graces of his life.

Tyburn, for one hundred and fifty years, from the reign of Henry VIII to that of Charles II, was the Calvary of our persecuted Church. It was also a place of pilgrimage, from the time that Saint Edmund Campion would go to salute the gibbet, on which one day he was himself to hang. Queen Henrietta Maria prayed beneath Tyburn Tree for the conversion of her adopted country, and Catholics of all ranks have ever loved to visit the spot and venerate the memory of the Martyrs whose blood had reddened the soil.

In the course of 1901, a zealous layman, Mr Dudley Baxter, was staying with me at Erdington Abbey, and we had long conversations as to the project, so dear to our hearts, of building a votive church or chapel as near as possible to the site of Tyburn Tree. It seemed to us such a terrible thing that we English Catholics should, as yet, have done nothing substantial to honour the memory of these heroes at the spot where they had poured out their blood. But there were obvious difficulties in the way. Situated as Tyburn is, close to the Marble Arch, in one of the most expensive quarters of London, how was it possible that we, in our poverty, could hope to erect there a shrine worthy of its cause? Nevertheless, we determined to pray without ceasing for this intention. We felt that God willed it, and that it must be granted us.

Mr Dudley Baxter, in fact, never passed by the site without raising his hat and praying to the Martyrs for this intention. I may quote what followed in Mr Baxter's own words.

'I think it was one autumn day, in 1901, not long after my return to London, that I was actually saying this little prayer, when something impelled me to look across the road. ... My eyes straightway lighted on a notice of a house for sale there, whereupon I at once recalled this idea which had seemed to me so hopeless. That evening I wrote to Cardinal Vaughan's chaplain, the Duke of Norfolk and Dom Bede Camm.'

The date of this event was the exact day that Mother St Peter and her daughters came to England and began their life at Bassett Road. The Mother had written through Père Lemius to the Cardinal to ask for certain authorisations. On the same day His Eminence's chaplain gave him Mr Baxter's letter, and suggested that the nuns from Montmartre might settle at Tyburn. Cardinal Vaughan was much pleased at the idea. Père Lemius, in his souvenirs of the Mother, continues the story. 'The Cardinal's secretary, a few days later, sent me the document I had asked for, and wrote with great kindness. In a post-script, he added: "His Eminence understands that there is a house for sale at the Marble Arch. He would be pleased if the Community could buy it and settle at this spot." Then came the words— "This is not an order which His Eminence gives, but a simple suggestion."

'This letter reached me at the Oblates' house at Kilburn, where I was lunching with Father James O'Reilly, the Superior. I asked him, "What is this Marble Arch?" "Why do you ask me that?" he said. "Look what the Cardinal says." I handed him the letter, which he read. He struck the table with a blow of his fist, and cried out, with extraordinary emotion, "It's too marvellous for words!" Then he explained to me that this place, one of the finest situations in London, is also the most sacred. It is Tyburn, the place where the English Martyrs suffered at the time of the Reformation, it is the Montmartre of London! "Ever since I became a priest," he added, "I never pass that spot without saluting the blood of our Martyrs, and asking God not to let me die until I have been able to say Mass there. It's now three centuries that this place has been sanctified, and up till now the Catholics have had no chapel there. All the religious in England are asking which Order will have the honour of building and serving this Sanctuary of these holy Martyrs. And now the Cardinal proposes that a Congregation of French nuns should found this chapel! I can't get over it!" "Then," replied I, "there must be no refusal." He got up, saying: "Let us go and see about it at once." We went together to communicate to Mother Mary of St Peter the Cardinal's "suggestion." The Mother remained silent for a while, in communion, no doubt, with the Sacred Heart, and then she replied, "Yes, I believe that God wills it." '

The house proposed by the Cardinal proved, however, to be unsuitable for a community. It was too small, and there was no garden. However, we set out immediately with the Mother to consult a Catholic solicitor, Mr Leathby. He explained to us that there were great difficulties against the project. If the Protestants knew of the plan, they would do all in their power to stop it, and then it was the part of London where house property was the most expensive. And the community found it hard enough to exist, especially in London.

It was agreed that the matter should be kept secret, and that they should await the succour of divine Providence. The solicitor was charged to look out for freehold houses for sale, and it was agreed that they must find a house possessing a garden.

On returning to the Community it was decided to pray ardently, and not to consent to the purchase until God, in His goodness, had sent them a sum of at least £10,000. The solicitor commenced his researches, the Community betook themselves to prayers, and the greatest secrecy was observed. Yet if the plan remained a secret, how would God grant us a benefactor? A month later Mr Leathby wrote announcing that he had at length succeeded in discovering at Tyburn a large house such as was needed, and that the price was as he had foreseen, no less than £15,000. This letter came at nine o'clock in the evening.

Now at six o'clock the same day, after the Benediction of the Blessed Sacrament, a young French lady went to see the Mother. She said: 'Some fifteen years ago, I received from an aunt, who lived in London, the sum of ten thousand pounds.' She explained to me that this sum had been paid to her by the English Government as compensation for the emancipation of their slaves in the South of Africa. 'When I knew the origin of this capital, which I used to call "the price of blood," I determined that I would not keep it, but would employ it in good works in honour of the Sacred Heart.' She added that she had often had the idea of giving it to me for Montmartre, but some interior voice always seemed to hold her back. The interest of the money had served meanwhile to help the good works carried on at the Visitation Convent at Orleans in honour of the Sacred Heart.

'But having heard the Mother speak of the project regarding Tyburn, she at once felt herself irresistibly impelled to apply the whole sum to this great work. She wished to remain entirely unknown. The emotion we felt, when three hours later came the letter from the solicitor, can be better imagined than described.'

The good Father then tells us that he found this lady was under the direction of Bishop Touchet of Orleans, afterwards a Cardinal, and that he went himself to Orleans to consult him on the matter. When he arrived the Bishop made a gesture of welcome and said: 'I have been informed, I have reflected. Take this sum of money, Father, it comes to you directly from Heaven.' He continued gravely: 'If you have any difficulties about it later on, refer them to me; I am your witness and your guarantee.' Thus the Bishop of Orleans, the devoted champion of St Joan of Arc, became one of the principal agents in the foundation of Tyburn Convent.

The nuns in their Chronicle add some interesting details:

'The views of Providence were manifest, but our Mother had only £20 towards buying an expensive house in an expensive neighbourhood. We began a Novena. On the seventh day a French lady, whom our Mothers had known only for a short time, and to whom she had spoken (not suspecting that this lady was in a position to give any pecuniary help), came to Mother and told her how she had for the last fifteen years had a certain amount of money, about 35,000 francs (equal, at that time, to about £9,400), which she had promised to the Sacred Heart to employ for His glory. That morning at Holy Mass she had seen clearly that she must give this money to her and her community for the purchase of the house at 6 Hyde Park Place, in honour of the Sacred Heart and the Martyrs of Tyburn.'

The French lady, whose name as she desired has remained a secret, was specially touched at the idea that Tyburn was destined to be in a double sense the Sanctuary of hearts, since there would be venerated the Martyrs, most of whom had had their hearts torn from their breasts for the love of Christ, and that there, too, the King of our hearts would be perpetually adored in the Sacrament of His love. She added that she knew that she could not give the whole cost of the house, but that she could, at least, give the greater part of it, and that she would pay over this sum whenever the Mother wanted it. And this, indeed, she did, a little later.

As a fact, the acquisition of the property and the considerable expenses necessitated by its repairs and the modifications needed to adapt it for the use of a Community, amounted to almost double the gift; but the will of God in all this appeared so manifest to Cardinal Vaughan, that he came himself to tell the Sisters of the great joy that these providential coincidences had given him, and assure them of the earnest desire he had to see the Tyburn project realised. Until his death, the Cardinal never ceased to encourage and favour the work.

The house that had been so providentially discovered, together with the two adjoining, had formed during the reign of Napoleon III, the French Embassy. Here Holy Mass was frequently offered in the Embassy Chapel. Here, too, was another coincidence, binding together England and France. Here, close to the spot where the French Queen of Charles I had made her pilgrimage, this house was purchased with the aid of French alms, to form a national Sanctuary for English Catholics, by French nuns who were vowed to perpetual prayer for the conversion of England. Later on the house had belonged to the Denman family, and here Father Philip Fletcher, who was to become one of the most devoted friends of Tyburn Convent, used to come as a little boy to play with the Denman children. One of them became a Catholic, and when she heard of the foundation, wrote to say how happy she was to think of her old home now becoming a house of prayer. This lady, Mrs Davis, has since become a benefactress of the Convent.

Père Lemius tells us that not long after this wonderful donation, the Mother came to him, greatly moved. 'See,' she said, 'I have just bought the *Life of Campion*. I opened the book by chance, and came on this wonderful prophecy made before the tribunal more than three hundred years ago. "Yes," said the accused, "I have said it, and I say it again, here before you. You have slain the greatest man in England. I will add that one day there, where you have put him to death, a religious house will arise, thanks to an important offering." '

This is the prediction already referred to.[1]

During 1902 took place the various transactions necessary for the purchase of the freehold. It became definitely the property of the Community in the month of August. But the various alterations took time, and they could not inaugurate the

---

[1] The account in the State Papers is as follows: 'The information of Richard Davison of Henley, Co. Oxon, tailor, taken before us, Sir Henry Newell, Knight, and William Knowles Esqre. at Henley beforesaid, the 8th day of June, 1585: Who saith as followeth that the 8th day of the said month, he and one William Wheteley being in a close at Henley town end, heard a couple talk, and repaired near unto them to hearken what they said. One of them he knew, whose name was Evan Arden of Henley aforesaid. ... Arden said unto one Gunne that was with him, "How can you praise Campion?" and Gunne answered again that he was the only man in all England. Then said Arden, "How can you praise Campion, being so arrant a traitor as he was?" Then answered Gunne, "Say not so, for the day will come, and I hope to see it, and so may you too, that there shall be an offering where Campion did suffer." Then said Arden, "What, shall we offer unto the Gallows?" "No, not so," said Gunne, "but you shall see a religious house built there for an offering." Gregory Gunne, priest, as we learn from the same State papers, was arrested on June 7, 1585, for these "traitorous speeches" (he had gone on to deny that the queen was Supreme Head of the Church, and to affirm the Petrine claims) and there was found on him "an Agnus Dei of silver with two consecrated Hosts within it, 11 beads of amber with a crucifix," etc. He was sent up for examination by the Privy council. He was born in Norfolk, studied at Magdalen College, Oxford, and had been beneficed at Elford in Oxfordshire. He had been ordained priest at Norwich in Queen Mary's reign. This is all I have been able to find about him.' (*Dom. Eliz.*, 179, 7, ff. 10, 14.)

new sanctuary until March of the following year.

Meanwhile, it may well be imagined what joy was given by the news of the purchase to the English Catholics who loved and venerated the memory of their Martyrs. I wrote to offer my congratulations to the Mother, while she was still at Bassett Road, and the letter she wrote me in return began a friendship which lasted till her death, and indeed, beyond. I possess hundreds of her letters, and if I do not quote from them, it is because her gracious kindness made her think too much and speak too warmly of the various little services that I was happy enough to be able to offer her, for love of the Martyrs to whose cause I had for long been devoted. As I got to know her more intimately and to realise what a great saint she was, my devotion to her became, as it were, a part of that already given to our Martyrs. She was, indeed, worthy to live on that sacred soil, she was a martyr herself in will, and, in fact, a great part of her life at Tyburn was a veritable martyrdom, as we shall see. And she knew how to inspire the same zeal, the same spirit of sacrifice, the same thirst for martyrdom in the hearts of her daughters. We shall find proof of this in the next chapter.

The nuns took possession of Tyburn Convent on March 3, 1903, and on March 6, the Feast of the Holy Lance and Nails, the first Mass was said there by Father O'Reilly, who thus obtained the answer to his prayer. This Mass was said in the Oratory of the Martyrs on the ground floor, as the chapel above was not yet quite ready.

However, on March 20, Feast of the Five Wounds, and eve of the Feast of St Benedict, the first Mass was said there by the secretary of Cardinal Vaughan, and Père Lemius preached a very remarkable sermon, which made a great noise in the Catholic press, and was by no means passed over by the Protestant journals. It showed that the aim of the Tyburn foundation was just what it is still, a work for the glorification of the Sacred Heart and of the English Martyrs, a work devoted to the conversion of the country which was known as an Island of Saints and Our Lady's Dowry.

chapter thirteen

A Time Of Trial

SINCE coming to England the Community had been increased by the reception of postulants, three of whom were English. This made them twenty in number. It was not yet possible with so few to inaugurate at once the perpetual Exposition of the Blessed Sacrament. But even now they began by giving five nights a week to Adoration.

It will be easily understood what a tax this was on the strength of a small Community. But they persevered, and at last their hopes and prayers were crowned with fruition. They were able to inaugurate the Perpetual Adoration by night and day before the Blessed Sacrament exposed on their altar on October 9, 1904. This day in France is the Feast of St Denis the Apostle of Paris, and the chief martyr of their dear Montmartre, while in England that year it was the Feast of the Maternity of Our Lady. Whilst at Bassett Road the Mother had written to a friend in Paris (December 26, 1902): 'We are 16 at present, but before February 24, when we move to Tyburn, I think we shall be giving the habit to three English postulants who have made themselves much loved here, and who are very fervent. They love us also very much. Thanks to God, then, all goes well; that does not prevent our having trials as you can well believe. But if we had none, I should think that our Dear Lord was turning His back on us.'

She herself was often suffering great pain and weakness. She writes on July 25, 1903, that she could scarcely find strength to go down to the chapel for Mass and Benediction, and she could remain up only for a part of each day. 'For us one thing alone is necessary, to see God's will and to accomplish it. It is for this that we must learn to live and die.' That, indeed, was the keynote of her life.

They had also heavy trials of another kind to bear. 'New evils threaten us at this very moment. In spite of these crushing trials, we remain calm and full of trust in the Sacred Heart. We work ceaselessly on behalf of the Community, who happy, peaceful and fervent, have no idea of the efforts hell is making to destroy it.' In fact, only the Mother, Mother Agnes and Mother St John were aware of what was pending, and their sole confidant was Père Lemius.

'Since we will absolutely all that He wills,' she continued, 'and desire to suffer all that may please Him to send us, since we desire that our life, our work, and our all should be totally consecrated to Him, and we have no other end than to accomplish His will, are we not assured that His grace is with us to hold us up, and that, if we are faithful, it will never desert us? After all, what happens is of little importance! The Martyrs of Montmartre and those of Tyburn knew how to suffer for the glory of their good Master. Their example must help us and give us courage.'

And very soon afterwards, on the Feast of the great Martyr St Lawrence (August 10, 1903), God asked a new sacrifice from the little Congregation, or perhaps, to put it more truly, it was asked to offer to Him its first martyr. This was Sister Mary Cécile, who was scarcely twenty years old. She was a younger sister of Mother Agnes, the Co-Foundress. In the month of May of the preceding year she had joined the Community, when her sister became her Novice-Mistress.

Her vocation had been a triumph of the Sacred Heart. She loved all that was beautiful, she was truly pious, but the world had for her many attractions. But the grace of God triumphed. She saw that for her it must be all or nothing. And generously, loyally she resolved to leave all to find her All. She grew rapidly in holiness. On the day she received the religious habit, she made, 'under the dictation of the Sacred Heart,' as the Mother expressed it, a special offering of her life for all the intentions of the Divine Heart, for all the nations of the world, especially for England and France, or any to which she might be sent.

A few weeks later she fell ill; and on the arrival at Tyburn, she had to take to her bed; where for some months she endured great sufferings, the origin of which were quite incomprehensible to the doctors. In May she received the last Sacraments, after which she had the happiness of making her vows and receiving the black veil of the professed. Yet she lingered on till the middle of August, always in a state of peace and happiness, absolutely abandoned to the divine Will. As she lay dying, her dear Mother read to her the act of offering which she had made, and though she could not speak, the expression on her face showed that she understood it, and ratified it.

Then the Mother Foundress offered to the Sacred Heart, this her first child, whom He had willed to receive as a victim. While she was saying the prayer, 'Wounded Heart of Jesus, be Thou opened to receive this soul,' the little Sister passed away. And many and many a time, the Community has recognised the effects of her help and intercession.

Tyburn soon began to draw devout souls around it. One of the greatest of its friends and benefactors was, as we have said, Father Philip Fletcher, the Founder, with Mr Lister Drummond, of the well-known Guild, of Our Lady of Ransom for the Conversion of England. The Mother loved to call him 'the Foster-Father of Tyburn,' and his devotion to Tyburn only increased with the years.

In May, 1903, he, with Father O'Reilly, organised the first pilgrimage to Tyburn, and it was destined to be the first of very many.

The present writer had this year the happiness of giving the first Retreat to the Community at Tyburn, November 15-23. After the Retreat was finished he was privileged to admit to Holy Profession three of the English novices. Among them was one who was to become perhaps the best known of all the Community, the late Mother Hildegarde.

We quote from a Notice in the Necrology of the Congregation: 'Her zeal and supernatural devotedness, added to her natural abilities, helped to bring the Congregation through many financial difficulties and won for it many friends both by her letters and personal relations with them. She worked for the success of the Quarant'Ore almost to the last, a fitting prelude to her death, which fell on the Feast of Corpus Christi (May 26, 1932). According to her desire, she was laid to rest by the side of Sister Marie Genevieve, her twin sister in religion, in St Benedict's little cemetery.'

In December, 1903, was celebrated a Triduum in honour of Saint Edmund Campion and Saint Cuthbert Mayne. The Mother, writing to me, says that the first two days the attendance was small (though most devout and fervent), on account of the bad weather; but that on the third day (December 1, the Feast of Saint Edmund) there was a great crowd, which greatly rejoiced the heart of good Father Fletcher.

In the following year there were, as there still are, two Triduums, with sermons, in honour of the Martyrs, one culminating on May 4, the Feast of the English Martyrs, the other on December 1.

The Mother continues: 'The Feast of Saint Campion brought us an unexpected consolation. Several priests wrote to ask leave to say the Mass of the Martyrs in our Convent. We had five Masses that day. Next year we hope we shall have a High Mass.'

In 1907, the Community had already so much increased that it numbered more English than French subjects. And now the pilgrims, too, who flocked to Tyburn, had so grown in number that the chapel had already become quite inadequate. Some day, in His own time God will, we feel certain, hear our prayers; and permit His children to raise at Tyburn a more worthy memorial to His Martyrs.

The finances of the Community were, at this time, in a desperate state. Our Lord often gave the Mother precious words of comfort, as she confided to Mother Agnes. Thus on November 15, during Mass, she was begging Our Lord to come to their aid, representing to Him that the Community was, as it were, suspended over an abyss. He replied to her: 'It is true, but I am holding you up. I will not let you perish, I promise it. You will have yet more difficulties, but all will be arranged.'

The very next day He seemed to say to her: 'I will come to your aid shortly.' And again He said to her: 'There will yet be other difficulties, but I will save you, have trust in Me.'

There were, indeed, other and far greater difficulties, coming. But as a Benedictine monk of La Pierre-quivire, who had known the Mother for many long years, wrote after her death: 'She was endowed with the gift of Fortitude to a heroic degree. ... To be heroic on one day of one's life, is possible, to be heroic perpetually, that passes the limits of human strength. I have asked myself a hundred times if Mother St Peter ever stopped on her way one single moment to tremble before what the future might bring. When God told her what He wanted of her (and I know that He did so tell her) she went forward, she did not hesitate a moment, and at last she arrived at that which Jesus had asked of her.'

And Dom Columba Marmion, Abbot of Maredsous, who took the Mother under his direction from 1908, never hesitated to speak of her as a great saint; and in 1913 he wrote of her to Mother Agnes: 'The special characteristic of your Mother is heroic confidence in the midst of impossibilities, and God wills that her children share this spirit.'

In fact, this heroic confidence was the Mother's strength, she knew that she could and must find all her support in the Sacred Heart of Jesus, who had asked this work of her; she was fully conscious of her poverty and her littleness, but this consciousness only increased her trust in Him who had pledged Himself to do all and give all, as long as she, on her part, did all she could.

It will be remembered that at the very beginning of the

foundation of Montmartre, she had made Mother Agnes kneel beside her in the Oratory at 'Nazareth,' and pray that they might have the grace of being always poor. Nevertheless, this poverty brought to them hours of indescribable suffering, for were they not responsible for the souls and the bodies of the children God had given them? But the Sacred Heart was ever with them to console and encourage them, and lead them safely through the most overwhelming difficulties.

I find noted in my diary (December 5, 1908): 'Called at Tyburn. The Reverend Mother in great financial distress. Does not know if they can remain at Tyburn as they have to borrow money every year to pay their interest, and have few or no benefactors. Very sad!'

But we find her writing to a friend: 'If you knew what a multiplicity of occupations and solicitudes devour our days! It is scarcely credible. Our supreme and incomparable consolation is that it is all for the good Master, whose Heart sustains, encourages and strengthens us. ... His love bears us up, so that we cannot succumb. Ah! how good it is to serve Him in the midst of this darkness through which we have to make our way. There seems always to be an abyss opening before us, which we have to cross; but hand in hand with the Beloved, we advance trembling, indeed, but still more filled with trust. And the abyss recedes, always recedes, and by the grace of the Sacred Heart we are saved from being engulfed within it.'

Here, indeed, as we shall see, is the secret history of Tyburn.

In a letter written to Abbot Columba Marmion (December 23, 1909), she gives an account of the state of her soul.

'I hardly know how to describe it, devoured as I am by material cares of the most agonising nature, not knowing what I can do, tortured by a continual anxiety which harasses me all day and allows me very little sleep at night: and yet I feel my soul calm and more at peace than ever before, even in the midst of cruel temptations against the Faith. I feel for my God a love that grows, that becomes stronger, that detaches me from myself and from everything, save in God and for God. ... I have had, and I still have, much to suffer from our terrible financial trials, from my own incapacity and powerlessness, from a host of other cares, and specially that of seeing myself often cowardly and unmortified. ... And at the same time, in spite of this humiliating burden of misery and worries, my soul dwells in her God, because He supports her, holds her up, carries her, sustains her in a life of faith, of love and confidence, not sensibly consoling, but supremely happy! It is difficult to explain a state so complex, as it were, a two-fold life, one natural, physical and sensitive, moral, too, in some degree, which is truly pitiable; and at the same time another supernatural, lifted up, alive with love, conformity and abandonment to the divine Will, rejoicing in tribulation, blessing God for the sufferings which He is pleased to send, and recognising with grateful joy that its most cruel trials are those which unite it the most to God.

'Father, I have no longer visions, nor that elevation of the soul to God by those transports that I used to have sometimes in contemplation. ... When I am too much overcome by these temporal difficulties, then my refuge is in the intimate union with Jesus on the Cross, in the most agonising moment of His life, of His Passion even, when He uttered that terrible cry: 'My God, my God, why hast Thou forsaken Me?' There, Father, I plunge myself in the distracted Heart of Jesus, and there I dwell. It is the culmination of His love, to have willed to know such suffering, to have willed even to be forsaken by His Father. Then this cry of His, I utter it with Him, it seems that I have faith no more, and yet I know that it is faith alone which makes me thus cry out! It is faith in Jesus, faith in His love, and in His whole-hearted devotion to His Father. And I understand vaguely that there we have the culminating point in the sufferings of Jesus, and that at that moment He saved us from despair, and caused us to make with Him the most perfect act of love and the most complete act of abandonment. I ought to tell you, Father, that these moments are frightful, and I hardly dare to think of them. ... And when they have passed by, the soul remains calm, reassured, more than ever God's, nailed to the Cross of Jesus, and ready to suffer all that He may will. It is the grace that flows from the tortures of Jesus.

'During these last two weeks, my God has shown me how mistaken I was in thinking that in reality I clung to Him alone, and put all my trust only in Him. He has shown me my illusions, and has revealed to me sacrifices yet to be made, and which were to me extremely difficult; but He has made me accomplish those which He has shown me.

'You told me, that while doing all in our power to keep Tyburn, I must be ready to make the sacrifice. I saw that this would cost me more than I imagined, and at the same time I shrank from the cares, the confusion, the derision, etc. etc. I then begged our Lord to help me to accept all that, and His grace disposed me to do so. No doubt I should find myself very cowardly when the trial came. ...

'I have also had to envisage the possibility, the probability almost, of the destruction of our little Congregation; the sacrifice that had to be made; not only for myself, but for Agnes, for all my daughters, and for each one of them, who love so tenderly their religious family. It was again terrible, but Jesus enlightened me as to each point and gave me the necessary grace.

'One thing still more intimate had yet to be done. My need of God, of being united to Him without interruption, without end, without cloud or veil, made me so sigh after Heaven that I had an ardent desire to die, to be with my Jesus, with my God!

'However, it seemed to me that while our religious family remained in these frightful financial straits, I ought not to desire to die, but on the contrary to live and bear this cross, to bear it for all my sisters. If such a catastrophe was to happen, I must ask God to let the grief and pain fall chiefly on myself, to let me

Adèle Garnier, aged 35

Marie Adèle in the first habit

The Oratory of the Martyrs

Above: the original resting place of Mother Adèle Garnier in Royston
Below: her final resting place at Tyburn

The centenary celebration around the tomb of Adèle Garnier

Mother Adèle Garnier

Above and Below: Tyburn Priory, Riverstone, Australia

Left and Below:
St Benedict's Priory, Cobh,
County Cork, Ireland

Left and Above: Monasterio Paráclito Divino, Guatapé, Colombia

Benedictine Monastery, Largs, Scotland

Left and Right: Tyburn Monasterio Puerta del Cielo, Vilcabamba, Ecuador

Tyburn Convent, London.

Tyburn Convent, London.

Tyburn Monastery, Bombay, South Auckland, New Zealand

bear the load of responsibility, of difficulties and humiliations. And then a supernatural light showed me that God had no need of me to bear all these things, that it was a presumption to wish to take them on my shoulders; and that besides, I should injure more than help, and that I could disappear from this world without anyone being the worse off.'

One day, in her simplicity, the Mother asked Our Lord to show what they ought to do if the Congregation should perish; and she heard this reply: 'But I do not will that it should perish.' And on another occasion, He vouchsafed to say to her: 'How can you be so anxious; should I allow this little Congregation to perish, which I have Myself founded?' And a little later: 'I will watch over you. I will make you come safely out of all these difficulties. Have trust in Me. You are working for Me. Courage!'

She had, indeed, need of courage, and we shall see how Our Lord sustained her in the trials that lay before her.

chapter fourteen

Tyburn's Crisis (1908-1911)

MEANWHILE Tyburn was becoming too small to house the growing Community, and it became necessary to think of making a new foundation. It was still impossible to think of France, but a providential visit of Cardinal Mercier directed their thoughts towards Belgium. Dom Columba Marmion, who was the close friend of His Eminence the Archbishop of Malines, and who had this very year become a devoted friend of the Mother and her Community, was the means of bringing the great Cardinal in touch with them.

In this year (1908) took place the Eucharistic Congress at Westminster, and Cardinal Mercier was pledged to attend it. Dom Marmion seized the opportunity of making known to His Eminence our little Community of Adoration, and even suggested to him that it would be most desirable that they should make a foundation in his diocese that they might there pray for his beloved Belgium.

The Cardinal was much interested in all he heard. Dom Columba told him that in his opinion the Mother was in all the world the most holy soul then living. He desired to know her, and asked that he might stay at Tyburn during the Congress. It was represented to him that the accommodation they could offer him was so very poor and miserable that it was quite unworthy of a Prince of the Church—there was, in fact, but one room generally used as a parlour-but he insisted—that he would prefer it to anything else. It was, as it turned out, an immense grace for the Community, for he became their devoted friend and helper. From that time, until his death, he was to them a true Father and friend.

He conceived an extraordinary reverence for the Mother Foundress, he saw in her a soul truly led by the Holy Spirit. But extracts from his own letters will best show what he thought of her.

He wrote from Malines, September 20, 1908, on his return:

'MY GOOD MOTHER,

'Though late, yet with all my heart I thank you once more for the kind hospitality which you have so graciously granted me, in your dear home at Tyburn. I did well to refuse certain offers made to me, however brilliant, for nowhere else could I have met with the devotion, the simplicity, the calm, the religious atmosphere which I had the joy of finding among you.

'...May the good Master to whom you are so wholly consecrated reward you.'

Again, he writes in December: 'I beg you to believe that I do not forget you before God. I beg Him to sustain you in your interior trials, to purify you more and more, and to give you an affection like that of St Teresa for Our Lord Jesus Christ.

'My journey to London will have been, thanks to your generosity, one of the richest spiritual favours of my life. Unhappily, my dear Mother, I may venture thus to confide in you—there is in my love for our dear Master more of desire than of will. I aspire, or rather He makes me aspire, after a union more close and more enduring with Him, but the world outside encumbers me, distracts me, and I feel myself growing old without directing towards Heaven anything but *hopes* for this union. Supply, I beseech you, for my insufficiency. It is to me a consolation to think that in your charity you are taking this burden upon you. I bless you with fatherly affection.'

These letters (and there are others later) show what the holy Cardinal thought of our Mother, while they cast a wonderful light upon his own humility.

It will be clear with what paternal affection and zeal he welcomed into his diocese the little foundation on which they were now engaged.

On January 3, 1909, the Mother with Mother Agnes, went to arrange about the foundation in Belgium. A house had been found at Koekelberg, a suburb of Brussels, not far from the site of the future Basilica of the Sacred Heart. The house was not too suitable for a Convent, and it was clear that before very long it would become too small.[1] But for the present it had to suffice. The Apostolic zeal of the Community at Tyburn rejoiced in the prospect of a new centre of prayer and adoration, but it involved at the same time a great sacrifice for those who were chosen to go there. They had to leave their Sisters, but most of all the Mother whom they so tenderly loved.

On their way to Brussels, the Mothers stayed with Joséphine Garnier, who had promised to give her furniture to the new Convent, and intended, if her health permitted, to live there as a boarder. But it was not to be. God called her to Himself on February 13, and thus the little Congregation lost a devoted friend and benefactress, and the Mother a most beloved sister. Before the departure of the Sisters for the new Convent, which was to be dedicated to Our Lady of Perpetual Succour, Dom Columba Marmion preached at Tyburn a Retreat to the whole Community. It made a great impression on them all. Indeed, those who have assisted at his Retreats well know that there was nothing to be compared with them. This was in April, and in June, the nine Sisters, who had been chosen for the new foundation, left for Belgium. Dom Columba said the first Mass in the Convent chapel on the Feast of the Sacred Heart, and enthroned the Blessed Sacrament. The chapel was henceforth open to the public. The chapel was furnished and decorated at the expense of an American benefactor, Mr Buckley. Mother

---

[1] In the year 1920 the Community moved to a larger house at Bierghes-lez-Hal in Brabant, which was opened on September 1.

Agnes had been named as Superior of the new Community, but she was only there till 1912, as her presence was too necessary at the Mother House. A noviciate for French-speaking Sisters was at the same time opened at the Koekelberg Convent.

This first foundation was a sign, hopeful and consoling, of the growth of the work to which the Mother had been called. But the future was by no means so comforting, and the very next year was to prove to the Mother and her little flock to be one of extraordinary difficulty and real anguish.

Tyburn itself was in danger; the financial crisis, which had so long been threatening, came to its climax, and to a soul less abandoned to God's will than that of our Mother, the future must have seemed one of absolute despair.

Owing to the seeming impossibility, humanly speaking, of struggling any longer against the increasing difficulties that had beset the Convent from the time of its foundation, it was decided that it was really impossible to remain on there, and that it must be given up. The cost of living, rates and taxes, etc., are very high in this part of London, and the mortages on the property amounted to no less than £11,757.

The following advertisement appeared in the Catholic papers, by permission of the Holy See.

'To be let or sold,

'6 Hyde Park Place, W., close to the Marble Arch. Tyburn Convent and Chapel, a substantial and roomy mansion, together with two gardens (freehold) and stabling (leasehold) within a few yards of the site of the Tyburn Gallows. Specially adapted for the wants of religious Community. The Community of nuns now residing there are compelled through pecuniary difficulties to leave, and desire to sell or let the premises to another Catholic Community or institution, so that the Sanctuary of the Tyburn Martyrs may remain open and its pilgrimages continue.'

It can be imagined what a bombshell this advertisement proved to all who loved Tyburn and its Martyrs. But what could be done? It seemed as if nothing less than a miracle could save the situation. By July this year, a Community of nuns was making offers for the Convent, and the Tyburn Sisters were packing up in preparation for their departure. They had even packed the books of their library.

But it was by no means settled where they would have to go. In June they had almost decided on a house near Birmingham, Stechford Hall. Then their thoughts turned to Belgium, and they inspected several houses at Louvain. But nothing proved really satisfactory, and, indeed, the bombardment and destruction that Louvain was so soon to suffer during the great war, would have made it a very perilous place of refuge. It was not really God's Will that they should be driven from their beloved Tyburn, though it seemed so at the time.

Dom Columba Marmion and Père Lemius both felt in their hearts that, in spite of all appearances, Tyburn would yet be saved. The Mother herself had written to Dom Columba, December 23, 1909, that she was tortured by continual anxieties which gave her no rest by day, and allowed her very little sleep by night; and yet her soul was in greater peace than ever before. She writes in July to Dom Marmion: 'As to Tyburn, our negotiations with the nuns of whom I spoke to you are prospering very well,[1] and I think that the business will be finally arranged in a few days' time. It is for us a great joy to adore in this affair the admirable designs of Our God. It was He Himself who established this work in the diocese, in spite of our poverty and nothingness; He has given us very much to suffer for His love, and now that the work of the pilgrimages is ripe for a greater extension, He gives it over to a Community much more fitted than ourselves to develop it to the greater glory of the Sacred Heart and to the honour of our Martyrs. Thus there are acts of thanksgiving which are mingled with the sacrifice.'

---

[1] The sale of the Convent to the Nuns of the Cenacle.

The present writer saw much of the Mother during this time. Her perfect peace, her joy in accepting the most cruel sacrifices, made an impression on him that can never be effaced.

But Our Lord did not intend this chosen soul to drink the chalice to the dregs. He willed that she should live and die at Tyburn, and He raised up friends and benefactors to make this possible. The friends of Tyburn rallied round the little Community and its beloved Mother. The Catholic papers were full of Tyburn and its terrible need. As I wrote at the time: 'God in His mercy intervened, and seemed to show clearly that this was His work, sealed with the marks of His Passion, and therefore doubly His. He willed, indeed, that His servants at Tyburn should suffer, but He did not will that their work should cease. When the public announcement was made, a thrill of sympathy and sorrow moved all hearts. It was felt it would be a real disgrace to Catholics of these days if a Sanctuary so sacred should be closed for want of public support, if the King of Martyrs should have to descend from His Throne at Tyburn and the ceaseless voice of pleading be silenced. Generous benefactors came forward at last, and banded themselves together to save this holy place.'

Benefactors came forward, from England, Ireland and France.

Mrs Stanley Cary promised to give £1000, on condition that others would promise the rest. Lady Mostyn of Talacre was indefatigable in her efforts to help, and she first suggested the idea that friends should subscribe to maintain a 'Sister of Prayer,' that is to say, to pay for the maintenance of a member of the Community who should devote her prayers to the needs and intentions of the benefactor. This idea was widely taken up, and Lady Mostyn herself had the privilege of having the Mother Foundress herself as her 'Sister of Prayer.' The Irish, who were then preparing for the beatification of their Martyr-Archbishop Oliver Plunket, were extraordinarily generous, and many most touching letters poured in, many of them from quite poor people, who sent their gifts with characteristic generosity. Other friends brought or sent gifts in kind. The Archbishop of Westminster was good enough to authorise a general appeal to English Catholics to save Tyburn.

This year saw the inauguration of the Great Novena to St Gregory the Great for conversions. More than 3500 names were sent in, and this has increased since then to really enormous proportions.

Another very important devotion was also inaugurated this year (1910) for the first time. This was the 'Walk from Newgate to Tyburn,' a procession along the road on which our Martyrs had been dragged to their death. This procession, which has assumed such vast proportions in later years, was begun by Father Fletcher and Mr Lister Drummond, the founders of the Guild of Our Lady of Ransom for the Conversion of England.

We have already alluded to the fact that even in penal times such processions were occasionally made. One such took place on Good Friday, 1624.[1] The writer, a bitter enemy of the Catholic religion, thus describes it.

'Yesterday being Good Friday, this present year, 1624, they made some of you in the morning before day, go in procession to Tyburn in penitential manner. ... But for the most part, your Processions in time and place of persecution as you call it, is nothing but a pilgrimage going barefoot or without shoes unto the sacred Shrine of Martyr-hallowed Tyburn. ... Would no other place serve to gad unto but Tyburn? Is no other place left sacred and unpolluted? Oh! but there is more virtue in the goal they run unto than in the race they undertake. It was ancient, to visit *Memorias Martyrum;* and so, the sending of Disciples to visit Tyburn, maketh a deep impression in their minds, of the saintship of some who have there paid their debt to our laws.'

---

[1] John Gee. *The foot out of the Snare,* p. 87. (London, 1624.) Gee was a notorious apostate. His book is now very rare. Five editions appeared in this one year.

Thus the apostate. But it is a precious testimony to the age-long devotion to our Martyrs. We read, too, in the life of Mother Margaret Hallahan, that as a little child she was taken to Tyburn, there to learn to walk. This was the custom of pious Catholic parents, so that their little ones might learn literally to walk in the steps of the Martyrs.

In 1911, gifts were still coming in.

Bishop John Vaughan made at this time a suggestion that was to bear great fruit, and do more than anything else to save the Convent. He suggested that as one hundred and five martyrs died at Tyburn for the Faith, if one hundred benefactors could be found who would give or collect the sum of 100 guineas (£105), the Sanctuary would be saved, and the mortgage paid off. The idea was received with general approbation, and it was decided that these benefactors should be known as the Founders of Tyburn, and that their names should be engraved on brass and hung in the chapel for perpetual remembrance. The Duke of Norfolk was one of the first to become a Founder, and the number grew as the years passed, until, although not yet complete, there are now over one hundred names commemorated.

But though it was hoped that the situation was now saved, there was still very much to be done. Meanwhile the nuns were suffering great privations. A priest, who was a special friend of the Community, asked the Sisters, on two separate occasions during the month of October, 1911, what they had had for dinner. The reply was the same. 'Onions and potatoes.' He then wrote to the *Universe*, in October, 1911: 'I happen to know how great the need is, how dire the poverty. Last week I found that these devoted nuns had had no food for several days but onions and potatoes. Surely there must be many who would like to help them, if they only knew the need?'

The response was truly astonishing. 'Hares and partridges,' to quote the Annals of Tyburn Convent, 'and provisions began coming in, and many letters enclosing contributions in money.

About £13, made up of small amounts, was received by one post. A girl offered to send us groceries every week. A poor woman sent one shilling, saying she could not bear to think of the nuns being in want, and this amount she would send every week that she was able to resist the temptation of spending it on drink.'

'The Mother Prioress, in thanking the priest for his letter, told him that they had had no idea he was going to sow onions broadcast over the 'Universe,' but that all the same, they were bringing in a flourishing crop. The *Te Deum* was sung in thanksgiving for this crop.'

The needs of Tyburn were also made known to the public in several pamphlets and articles published at this time: 'Tyburn Leaves,' 'Tyburn and the English Martyrs,' 'Tyburn speaks,' were the titles of some of them. They had a large circulation.

The Mother Foundress, writing to Dom Marmion (who had become Abbot of Maredsous in 1909) on December 28, 1911, thus describes the state of her soul during these trials. 'My dear Father, the heavier the cross, the more will Jesus bear it with us, and our troubles and labours will become our consolation, even when we feel crushed by them! In my own humble sphere, I experience this intensely. Sometimes it is as if I had to walk on ground that trembled under my feet, sown with thorns and briars; burning coals and yawning gulfs on every side of me. And yet I find myself, as it were, carried by Our Lord, so that I traverse without danger and without fear these multiplied obstacles. ...

'Our affairs at Tyburn remain still in the *status quo,* in abandonment, in the midst of the unknown. Mother Agnes says that our Lord is leading us on, bearing us up, as He did the Israelites in the desert. He keeps us at Tyburn by repeated miracles, which force us to remain on this way of expectation, but we do not yet see the promised land, that is to say, the future is not yet assured to us. We have to go on marching, camping out, as it were, and always He provides for our subsistence, for our needs, by His admirable Providence.'

chapter fifteen

St Benedict And His Children

IN 1912-13 the Oratory of the English Martyrs, on the ground floor of the Convent, was decorated. Though only a moderate-sized room, it now became a shrine of very great beauty. Over the altar was erected a model of the Triple Tree of Tyburn. From it were hung beautiful and costly lamps, crowned with diadems, in honour of the Martyrs. The Tree serves as a canopy to the altar which stands beneath it. The reredos was carved by the students of St Joseph's School of Arts and Crafts, attached to the great Benedictine Abbey of Maredsous in Belgium. They also executed the lamps, and embroidered the magnificent silk curtains which hang on the wall behind. Seven statuettes, carved in oak, adorn the reredos. In the centre is Our Lady as Queen of Martyrs. The others represent St John Houghton, the Protomartyr, Prior of the London Charterhouse, B. Sebastian Newdigate, another Carthusian Martyr, St Edmund Campion, S.J., St Ralph Sherwin, B. Thomas Sherwood, a layman, and St Richard Reynolds, the 'Angel of Syon.' These statuettes are designed with real religious feeling by a monk who has studied the Martyrs' lives upon his knees.

The curtains are magnificently embroidered with palms and crowns, and above are the coats of arms of England, Wales, Scotland and the Universities of Oxford and Cambridge. At the same time two beautiful stained-glass windows were designed to light the chapel. They represent, the one the eight Beatitudes, and the other the Seven Works of Mercy as illustrated in the lives of the Martyrs. They were the work of Miss Margaret Rope, now a Carmelite nun. A very competent critic, himself an artist in stained glass, once assured the writer that he considered them the very best stained glass that had been executed in England in our time. They must be studied minutely. Added to all this, the chapel was adorned with some beautiful pictures of the Martyrs, and enriched with very many of their sacred relics. It can well be imagined what joy this gave to the Mother Foundress, who was herself no mean artist.

The crucifix and candlesticks for the altar were designed specially for the shrine, and they may be said to reproduce the best examples of medieval days. The greater part of the cost of all this decoration was born by a devoted lady, an Oblate of St Benedict. As she has now passed to her reward, her name may be revealed. Miss Gwenllian Capel Miers. She was absolutely devoted to Tyburn and the Martyrs, and the Mother Foundress had a special affection for her.

The statuettes of the reredos were, however, given by various benefactors, including the Carthusians of Parkminster and the Bridgettine nuns of Syon Abbey. The work was not completed till 1913, and since that day many treasures, especially relics, have been added to the shrine. In the chapel upstairs, where the Blessed Sacrament is exposed night and day, the brasses upon the walls already bore the names of twenty-seven Founders.

In 1913 there was to occur a great sorrow to the Community and its friends, followed by a great consolation.

On March 21, which is the Feast of St Benedict, but was that year Good Friday, the Mother Foundress fell suddenly ill, and the illness seemed to be a hopeless one. She was seized with this malady during the Office of Matins. On the Wednesday in Easter week she seemed to be at death's door, and the doctor said that she must receive the last Sacraments immediately. She received them with her customary serenity.

'One day,' writes Mother Agnes, 'seeing me in a state of anguish, she called me near her and told me not to be afraid, for she was not going to die. Our Lord had warned her at the first seizure that she would be sick unto death, but she said, "I shall not die yet, the Sacred Heart has revealed to me that He has

deigned to hear the prayers which are being offered for me."
She felt the effect of these prayers fall on her like a dew from
heaven. And yet I could not bring myself to believe that she
would recover, she was so terribly ill.

'During the night of March 28 to 29 she passed two hours
in the most terrible sufferings. This was before midnight. At
last, seeing she grew calmer, I extinguished the light, and I
retired for a little to my cell, which is close to her own. When
she was left alone, she was once more a prey to paroxysms of
coughing.

'Suddenly, she saw a gentle light appear in the darkness
of the room, at a certain distance from the foot of the bed. In
the midst of this light, which was raised some four or five feet
above the floor, she saw a saint of majestic appearance. The
first instants of surprise having passed, she felt certain that it
was St Benedict. The Saint wore a woollen cowl, undyed, the
top of the head was bald, the features very delicate, the beard
long. A circle of gold, of two fingers' breadth, surrounded the
head, and the interior of this nimbus was full of light. The Saint
looked at our Mother with an indescribable expression, at once
serious, benevolent and full of peace. The right arm was folded
and hid something, while it remained in shadow, as did the
right shoulder. The rest of his person was in the light. With his
left hand, stretched out, he pointed to an illuminated sphere, of
which the light was increasing and spreading. He did not speak,
but he encouraged our Mother by his look to suffer in peace,
and to have great confidence for herself, for the Congregation
and for the future.

Our Mother understood that the luminous sphere to
which the Saint pointed, and which seemed to proceed from
him, signified the designs of God confided to St Benedict, in
which the Congregation would have its share, but which did
not concern it uniquely, for these designs were very vast. She
thought that it portended a great diffusion of the Faith and
the Christian and religious life in England and even beyond
England.

As to the object hidden beneath his right arm, our Mother had the impression that it signified some special grace that was held in reserve for our own religious family, but she did not understand what this might be.

'Filled with confusion and thankfulness, she flung herself in spirit on her knees at the Saint's feet. She felt quite timid, "just like a little girl," as she repeated to us several times. She did not dare to greet St Benedict out loud with the name of Father, but she murmured very low: "Our Father!" and then added, aloud, "St Benedict, pray for us!"

'The Saint remained there three or four minutes, as far as our Mother could judge, and then disappeared, leaving with her a sweet impression of peace, trust and gratitude, and at the same time an assuagement of her physical sufferings.

'Next day, as she thanked St Benedict for having granted her this consolation, which she was far from expecting, it seemed to her that the Saint invited her to do all she could for the incorporation of her Congregation into his Order, and assured her that he, on his side, would do what was necessary. But this assurance was rather under the form of an interior impression received in prayer. As to the vision, it had been so clear, so bright and so unexpected, that our Mother could not have the least doubt of its reality. She was wide awake at the time, and when the vision appeared, she was thinking neither of St Benedict nor of anything in particular, since she was in a state of great physical suffering, and half-suffocated by the cough.'

From midnight on April 1, which that year was kept in the Order as the transferred Feast of St Benedict,[1] she became quite notably better, and on the evening of April 2, the doctor declared her to be out of danger.

From the end of July till October the two Mothers were

---

[1] The Feast is on March 21, but as that year it occurred in Holy Week, it had to be transferred till after Low Sunday.

in Belgium. On their return, the Mother Foundress announced that the serious question of their official adoption of the Rule of St Benedict had been most carefully studied, and that she had decided to convoke a General Chapter to consider the whole matter. Meanwhile, the various monastic customs proper to the Order of St Benedict (that is those that were not already in use among them), were adopted in the two Convents of the Congregation.

The present writer, some time later, had the privilege of hearing the Mother relate to him this vision of our holy Father. He was admitted by special privilege to her cell, for she was not then able to come down to the parlour, and he will never forget as long as he lives, the description which she gave him of her vision.

The Chapter met on January 17, 1914. It must be remembered that when they were still in Paris, the Foundress and her first daughters had asked Cardinal Richard's permission to adopt the Rule of St Benedict as the type of perfection and base of their religious life, with the modifications that were made necessary by the requirements of their special vocation. This was granted them, and these Mothers had been authorised to make their perpetual vows, 'according to the Rule of St Benedict.' However, later on, when they were in England, doubts were raised if it were permissible to pronounce these vows according to a Rule written for an independent Abbey, since they felt that for them it was essential to be a Congregation formed of various houses, linked together under the rule of a Mother General. While awaiting the solution of this difficulty it was thought best that the nuns should make their profession according to the Constitutions, in which, of course, there were incorporated the principles and spirit of the Rule, as far as was compatible with their special vocation.

The Mother wrote to me from Tyburn, soon after their establishment there, a letter which may here be quoted. It is dated October 17, 1903.

'I am sending you to-day, dear Reverend Father, the MS. book of our Constitutions. … You will find in them many passages which breathe the spirit of St Benedict, which will not surprise you if I tell you that the Rule of St Benedict is the foundation of our own religious life, and that as far as was possible, with our vocation, we have been inspired by its spirit for our formation and in the drawing up of our Constitutions. It is no doubt a far-off resemblance, but we hope all the same that you will recognise in them a certain family likeness. For we have been anxious to follow the Rule of the Blessed Father in every point compatible with our vocation. And if we have St Gertrude as our very special Patron we also look on the Blessed Patriarch as our own Father. His Rule from the very beginning, and in an ever-increasing measure, as we have studied it more and understood it better, has been the ideal on which we would model our lives as closely as possible.'

When the nuns entered into relations with Dom Columba Marmion, the whole question was carefully gone into both by him and others, from the point of view of Canon Law and at the same time of the Benedictine Rule. Soon it became clear that there was really no obstacle to the accomplishment of their wish to be numbered among the children of the Holy Patriarch. They discovered that it was quite possible for them to follow the Rule, in a measure much more complete than they had at first imagined, without in the least degree affecting their special observance.

Besides, it was made clear that in all the Benedictine Congregations, when the Rule and the Constitutions differ as to certain points of observance, it is always the Constitutions which have the force of Law.

This was a great joy for the Mother Foundress, who had always felt such an affection for this holy Rule. Abbot Marmion himself presided at the Chapter, at the close of which (it being proved that the two Communities were unanimous in desiring to become Benedictines), he took the Acts of the Chapter to His Eminence Cardinal Bourne. He returned with the good news that the Cardinal had immediately confirmed the Acts. They were sent to Cardinal Mercier, who was equally pleased to confirm them.

One of the most striking consequences of this adoption of the Rule was the change of the religious habit hitherto worn by the nuns. About a month after the Chapter, they left off the white tunic, blue girdle and red scapular which up to then they had worn, and were clothed in the black Benedictine habit, though they still retained the white cowl in sign of their Eucharistic vocation. This cowl is worn in choir, and at the Adoration.

On February 16, the Sisters solemnly renewed their vows, 'according to the Rule of St Benedict and the Constitutions of the Congregation.'

Thus the vision of the Monastic Patriarch vouchsafed to the Mother, bore its fruit, and her children may now truly address the Saint as 'Our holy Father St Benedict'; since the Congregation so recently founded now became an integral part of the most ancient of all religious Orders.

It should have been added that the new Constitutions which were necessitated by this change, were finally drawn up and sent to Rome not long after the death of the Foundress. They were returned with the approbation of the Holy See in July, 1930, and thus this great grace vouchsafed to her was confirmed by the high authority of the Catholic Church.

St. Benedict has fulfilled his promise, that if the Mother would do what she *could* for their incorporation into his Order, he himself would do *what was necessary*. The Mother Foundress and Mother Agnes went over to Belgium in May, 1914, to see about finding a new house to replace the Convent at Koekelberg, which was already becoming too small for the growing Community. But they returned to Tyburn on July 21, for the great European war was on the point of breaking out.

On August 20, the Feast of St Bernard, the Holy Pope, Pius X, died in the odour of sanctity. His last recommendation to the

Catholics of the whole world was to make public supplication, so that the merciful God may, as it were, be wearied with the prayers of His children and speedily remove the evil cause of war, giving to them that rule, to 'think the thoughts of peace and not of affliction.'

A few days later, on the 27th, the Mother became so ill, that the doctor had to be sent for twice during that day. It was after invoking Pius X, and wearing a piece of his cassock, given to her by one of her nuns, that a decided change for the better took place, and she was pronounced out of danger. It may well be imagined how the horrors of the great war afflicted her gentle soul. Refugees came in large numbers, among them the sister-in-law of Cardinal Mercier, with her three sons, all of them seminarists. It was supposed that the sisters from their Belgian Convent might be expected at any minute; but they were allowed to remain on at Brussels.

August 16 brought a distinguished refugee. There suddenly appeared at the grille Abbot Columba Marmion, disguised as a Dutch cattle-dealer in check suit, blue shirt, green tie and round cloth cap! (He used to say himself that he had escaped, disguised as a jockey!) The sister at the Portress's Office mistook him for one of the builder's men. On entering, he forgot he was not wearing his ring, and gravely presented his finger to be kissed, making the sister imagine she had to do with a madman.

However, he was soon recognised under his bizarre disguise. He told them that he had encountered many dangers and only narrowly escaped being shot, as he was closely searched and was found to be carrying important papers. He had no passport. When he was asked for one on this side of the Channel, he replied that he was an Irishman, and that an Irishman only needed a passport for hell. One of the first things he thought of was getting his photograph taken, that it might find a place in the Archives of his Abbey. He had come over to find a place of refuge for his monks.

On September 26, seven of the sisters of St Mary's arrived

at Tyburn. No news of the rest of the Community came until well on in November. They remained on in their Convent, and were almost miraculously preserved during the perils of the war. On the Feast of St Thomas of Canterbury, Mother Agnes put a notice on the blackboard: 'If you hear the sound of firing (from the anti-aircraft guns), keep quite calm, which is surely easy with Jesus in our midst, and go down to the basement— except, of course, those who are at the Office or at Adoration, who will be delighted to risk something for the service of their King.'

Before 1915 was half over, it was noted that between fifty and sixty refugee Priests had come to Tyburn within the eight months of the war. Religious, too, of both sexes had come in great numbers. In ministering to these importunities, the Community would certainly have had to go on short commons if it had not been for the generous help supplied by the Belgian Refugee Fund. On June 15, 1916, God asked a very great sacrifice from the Mother and her Congregation, He willed to call to Himself the soul of one of the first companions of the Foundress, Mother Mary of St John of whom we have already spoken under her name of Alexida. She was a soul of extraordinary sanctity, and had drunk to the very dregs the cup of suffering. While her humility and simplicity might cause these graces to be unsuspected, none who met her could be unconscious of her love of God and of all that concerned His interests and glory, and, indeed, her generous devotedness and utter selflessness endeared her to all who knew her. She had held several important offices in the Community, among them those of Novice-Mistress and Infirmarian.

God sent her great sufferings during the latter years of her life, the greatest being the necessity of having to live and die outside her own Convent. She fell into consumption after undergoing a severe operation, and had to be sent to divers Convents and Homes in the country—all treatment proved of no avail, but wherever the divine Will led her, she did a great work for God by her gentle influence, religious fervour, and loving abandonment to the divine Will. In one of her last letters, she wrote to a Sister at Tyburn: 'All the sickness Our Lord has sent us this year is the answer to the offering of ourselves as "reparatrices" for the sins of the world. Never has poor humanity needed so many prayers and penances. If only after this dreadful war God would be loved more by men! We will do all we can for that, dear Mother, some in the active way, others in the passive. ... Our Lord is good, for He always gives graces to bear the trials he sends. If I had known beforehand all that was going to happen to me, I should have fainted of *frayeur*, but the ways of God are sweet.'

She died at Aubigny near Poitiers, being then in the fortieth year of her age and the eighteenth of her religious profession. She had received the last Sacraments, and in her longing for Heaven, she had been often repeating: *'Mourir, quel bonheur! on est si bien avec le bon Dieu.'* Her holy death gave rise to a great and spontaneous manifestation of veneration. Priests and people, religious and school children, not only of the place where she died, but from the whole surrounding neighbourhood, thronged to see her as she lay dead, and to attend her burial. They cried: 'The Saint is dead, the Saint is dead!'

I find among my notes some records of conversations with this devoted soul, and with the Mother Foundress about her. 'Mother St John has been raised to the prayer of union and seems enwrapped in God. Can do nothing but let Him carry her in His arms. Has visions of the demon, sometimes as a man, very beautiful, at other times most terrible. The other day (this was in 1903) she saw him in a transport of fury, blaspheming God, because, he said, he had lost a soul that belonged to him. This soul had once been holy, but had given up the Sacraments and so had fallen into the power of the Evil one. She has the most terrible combats to endure for souls. The other day, after seeing the devil and hearing his cries of rage, she heard Our Lady telling her that she must pray much for the soul of the

King (Edward VII) and confide it especially to the care of St Joseph.

'She is extraordinarily humble, and sometimes says she feels her own misery so acutely that she is tempted to leave the Community altogether. In prayer she feels an intense longing to suffer, a desire to be martyred for the love of Jesus, to be cut in pieces for Him, with the intention that He may be known and loved by all men. She tells all her graces and all her trials quite simply to the Reverend Mother, and puts herself absolutely in her hands.'

Her vocation was extraordinary. One day, Mother Agnes had a dream, in which she saw Père Chambellan, the Mother Foundress's great friend and director, who said to her: 'God will bless your undertaking, have courage and begin, but Mlle N., on whom you count, will not be with you; God has chosen another to take her place. She is very dear to Him. 'She wrote this to the Foundress, who was then in the country, waiting to start the Community. Here she had met Alexida, as she was called, who intended to become a religious, and had, indeed, been accepted by the nuns of the Immaculate Conception of Lourdes.'

The Reverend Mother felt a strong attraction to Alexida, and one day, when she knelt next to her at Holy Communion, she felt in her heart that God intended her to help to found the work. But she said nothing. Then Mlle N. wrote to say that her director would not allow her to join the foundress. So she went to Paris, and waited for the third person who was necessary in order to begin. And in a few days came a letter from Alexida, who had determined to throw in her lot with them. Thus divine Providence gave to the Foundress this devoted soul who was to be known as Mother Mary of St John.

She offered herself later as a victim for the conversion of England. And now God has crowned her sacrifice and taken her to her eternal reward.

chapter sixteen

St Benedict's Priory

I will here quote from the Annals of Tyburn, a MS. drawn up by the nuns year by year.

'This is not the place to tell the story of the foundation at Royston, and the manifest intervention of St Benedict in this matter. About the middle of 1915, a large picture entitled "The Benedictine Apostles and Martyrs of England,"[1] was hung in the Oratory of the Martyrs. It was painted by Sister Catherine Weeks, O.S.B., one of the convert Benedictines of St Bride's Abbey, Milford Haven, and represents St Benedict with his illustrious sons, St Gregory the Great and St Augustine of England, together with the English Benedictine Martyrs, the Blessed Mark Barkworth, George Gervase, John Roberts, Maurus Scott, Alban Roe, Philip Powel and Thomas Pickering, who all suffered at Tyburn for the Faith.

'A few days later Dom Bede Camm happened to meet Mgr Barton Brown in or near Piccadilly and, telling him he was going to Tyburn to see this new picture (the gift of Miss Miers), he asked the Monsignor to accompany him. This invitation was gladly accepted.

'It was Mgr Barton Brown's first visit to Tyburn, and Mother Agnes came down to receive him. The subject of the urgent necessity of a new foundation was spoken of, and Monsignor at once suggested that one should be made at Royston, near Cambridge (the mission that boasted of possessing two Catholics), that had recently been confided to him by Cardinal

---

[1] A print of this beautiful picture forms the frontispiece of my *Nine Martyr Monks*, published by Burns Oates & Washbourne in 1931.

Bourne, soon after the visit of the Motor-Chapel to that part of Hertfordshire. He wanted a contemplative Order in his parish. That part of England was so very Protestant and a Convent where the Blessed Sacrament would be constantly exposed and adored, would be a source of many graces. ... Mother Agnes went at once to Mother Foundress who was ill at the time and told her what Mgr Barton Brown had just said. Already many places had been suggested for this foundation. But Mother Agnes was struck at seeing how this one seemed to appeal to our beloved Mother Foundress, and she returned with this good news to the Monsignor.'

A few days later, Mother Agnes and Mother Hildegarde went to Royston to visit the two houses about which Mgr Barton Brown had written. One was a large house, beautifully decorated. It was called 'The Old Palace,' and once was part of the hunting lodge which King James I had built. The other was an unpretentious house with a pleasant but rather small garden.

Mother Foundress herself went a few days later, with Mother Agnes, to visit these houses. Dom Bede accompanied them, or rather met them at Royston. The Mother found the Old Palace much too grand for a few poor nuns, but she fell in love with the other, '*la petite maison pauvre,*' as she joyfully called it. And the price was only £1,100. It was on her birthday (August 15) that she made this visit, and she decided to take it as a sign of God's will concerning this house, if someone were to offer sufficient money to buy it.

Shortly before this, a lady had written to Tyburn, sending a gift of £50, and asking for prayers. She wanted light to know how best to spend a sum of money which she had promised to Our Lady of Lourdes to promote the Faith in Great Britain. She was written to, and came to Tyburn on August 18.[1] On hearing about the house, she offered to buy it, as soon as she was

---

[1] Her name was Miss Coats. At first, she wished to remain anonymous.

satisfied that the Convent Chapel was open to seculars, and that there was the possibility of a kitchen garden. She gave the price of the house and £300 in addition for repairs. Thus in three days the Mother Foundress's prayer was answered, and God's will was made known. When the Co-Foundress visited *la petite maison pauvre,* they had been struck by a large park adjoining it, and Mother Agnes having remarked how lovely it would be to have a part of that park to enlarge the garden, the Mother said they must pray and hope, and this might come to pass before long.

And so it did! In December, Mgr Barton Brown wrote that this property, consisting of a large modern house with the park, was for sale; and that the Sisters of Providence from Namur, who had been invited by the indefatigable Monsignor to come there to found a school, thought of purchasing it. They would be very pleased to come to an agreement with Tyburn, in the sense that they would purchase the house and the grounds at the upper end of the estate, and let Tyburn purchase that part of the park which adjoined their garden. This part of the grounds was valued at £1,100. Miss Coats kindly offered to give half this sum and lend the rest. Ultimately she gave the whole sum.

The opening of the new Foundation had to be postponed till December, 1916. It was called St Benedict's Priory. During the Octave of the Immaculate Conception; the inauguration of the new Convent took place. Eight nuns formed the Community, which was presided over by Mother Dominica as Prioress. The chapel was solemnly opened for public worship on December 12. Pontifical High Mass was sung by Bishop Butt. After the Mass the Blessed Sacrament was solemnly exposed, and thus Our Lord took possession of the new Eucharistic Throne prepared for Him.

In September, Cardinal Bourne had blessed the foundation stone of the new parish church, which is not far off the Priory. In his sermon he spoke of the coming of the Sisters of Providence. He then went on to say: 'But more important perhaps than even their coming, is the choice made by a Sisterhood devoted to prayer of intercession and reparation, to set up in this place their noviciate, and to have here also a community in which the younger members of the institute are to be trained. The Catholic Church has ever brought before you as part of her constant teaching the necessity of prayer; that all our work depends not on ourselves, but on God alone; that God will give us His help and assistance in proportion to the earnestness of our supplications: and that it should be granted to this town of Royston to have within its limits a religious sisterhood, whose one and only object is to make reparation, to make supplication, to spend a life in prayer, is a great blessing of the Providence of Almighty God for which the Catholics of this town cannot be too grateful, and which I trust non-Catholics will come to appreciate more and more as time goes on.'

It was not until the spring of 1919 that this beautiful church was opened. It was based on that of Santa Brigitta in the Piazza Farnese at Rome. Thus even in the midst of the great European war, the work of God went steadily on.

The Sisters at Royston must have been thankful for the tranquillity they enjoyed, after the cruel experience of Tyburn. Night after night bombs were cast on London from the Zeppelins and aeroplanes, and too often the Convent was rocked to its foundations, as one of the nuns wrote at the time: 'It is natural to feel that it matters little whether we are blown to heaven one of these nights, so long as no harm comes to the Blessed Sacrament, and also we know that the Congregation cannot be destroyed by all the aeroplanes in the world, so that it is quite easy to keep calm and cheerful. *Non timebo mala quoniam tu mecum es.*[1] Naturally speaking, there is every reason to be afraid. The crashing of shells overhead is truly terrific, the missiles whistle maliciously as they fly through the air, and the vibration is formidable. The upper parts of the house on

---

[1] 'I will fear no evil, for thou art with me'

these occasions rock like a storm-tossed ship, and it feels quite uncanny to walk up or down the upper flights of the staircase.'

The Office went on as tranquilly as if all was peace around them, only at its end special prayers were recited for the dead and dying, the injured, and for those who were causing so much havoc. They repeated the Salve Regina, the Litany of Loretto, the Rosary, the Parce Domine, 'and most pleasing of all to the Professed, Novices and Postulants alike, was the singing of the *Suscipe*[1] with arms extended in supplication and entire abandonment to the good pleasure of the Spouse.'

And what about the Mother Foundress? We read in the Annals: 'Our dear Very Reverend Mother alone can state that the raids had not cost her a single heartbeat, and her peaceful presence is another influence of hope and confidence felt by all her daughters in these stirring times.'

On October 7, in the midst of these alarms, she confided to Mother Agnes that during Holy Mass that day, she had twice seen Our divine Lord showing to her His Heart. He said to her: 'I will be with you always.' No wonder, then, that the air-raids left her in perfect peace.

To finish what we have told of the foundation of Royston Priory, we may have recourse to the memoirs of Mother Agnes.

'December 29, 1920, took place the transference of the Novitiate from Tyburn to Royston. From the beginning of its foundation it had always been intended to construct our Novitiate House there, but we were prevented by our poverty. Our dear Mother Foundress, however, was full of confidence, and assured her Assistant that we ought to have enough faith in the Sacred Heart to know that He could work miracles which would be in accord with Canon Law, which no longer permitted one to make a new foundation or an important construction without having the necessary funds in hand. The

---

[1] The *Suscipe me Domine* is sung by Benedictines at their profession.

confidence of our Mother was not deceived and the money came to us from a quite unexpected channel. It came through a Benedictine monk, who had long been devoted to Tyburn. We shall understand in a moment the explanation of this fact apparently so strange.

'Nine Novices under the care of their Mother Mistress made the journey thither.

'The Vigil of the Epiphany (January 5, 1921) was the day chosen for the solemn opening, and the benediction of the new Noviciate. Our generous benefactor preached on this occasion. Referring to the history of the Magi, their coming to Bethlehem with their gifts, he exhorted the Novices who were come to be trained in this Bethlehem—this House of Bread— to give to Our Lord the same offerings: "The gold, that is to say all that you have, all that you are, everything: the incense, that is the worship of God, your whole life must not be less than that; and lastly the myrrh, for you must suffer as your Saviour has suffered, and the Cross must be carried every day until the end." He finished by these words: "To-day I ask your prayers for the benefactor who has given you this Novitiate House-my Father. You may well ask how a monk, who has made the vow of poverty, can give anything, since he has nothing at all. My father, who was a very fervent convert, desired to give a part of his fortune to help on the work of the Church in England, and that is why he left a certain sum of money to that one of his sons who had no need of money for himself. At the moment of my profession I had naturally the duty of making my will, so that normally speaking this legacy should not have come to you till after my death; had it not been for the fact that my Abbot gave permission that this sum should be utilised at once, and given over to you. In consequence I ask your prayers for my father who gave the money, and for my second father, the Abbot, through whom you now receive it." '

The sum given was £3000, and with it the architect, Father Benedict Williamson, succeeded in erecting a lofty and spacious building, with a cloister attaching it to the Chapel and Priory. It was visited about this time by His Eminence Cardinal Gasquet, who was then staying at Benet House, Cambridge, for the Bible Congress.

On October 18, the Feast of St Luke, in 1921, 'the Monastic Breviary, closed down so far as public choir services in London is concerned, was, through a special favour of the Sacred Heart, taken up by the hands of His Adorers.[1] In our humble little chapel at Tyburn, where so many of St Benedict's sons offered their lives for the glory of God and of His Church, the form of prayer familiar to their lips is now established.

'Our Very Reverend Mother, to everyone's joy, was able to assist at this first office of Tierce. The radiance on her beloved face told sufficiently that a long desire was now satisfied, and the fruits of years of prayer repaid. Our Holy Father St Benedict also gave several tokens of his good pleasure and approval.'

---

[1] Up to now they had used the Roman Breviary.

chapter seventeen

The Last Years

As the years went by, the Mother Foundress's sufferings increased and became almost continual. In 1920 she was already eighty-two years old, and the last time she had been able to leave the Convent was when she went to Royston in 1915, June 24-July 2, to make the canonical Visitation. She remained almost constantly in her cell, having even to sacrifice, sometimes for long months together, the happiness of hearing Mass. But her one joy was to submit herself to the divine Will.

Her cell was like herself, poor and simple, but full of divine peace. Her children found her ever ready to receive them, and to gaze on her face welcoming them with her sweet motherly smile was enough to give them peace and consolation. She interested herself in all their little troubles, in their families, in their occupations. She, above all else, was interested in their spiritual advancement, and when it was necessary she knew how to reprove or correct with a sweet and penetrating firmness. They never left her, they declared, without feeling stronger, better able to see everything from the supernatural point of view. It seemed that there they learned to understand the value of abandonment to the divine Will. No one who heard her could ever forget the ecstatic tone in which she would pronounce the words: 'Oh! The Will of God, my child... if one only knew what it is! Oh! how we must love the Will of God!'

She had one great earthly comfort, and that was in the faithful devotion of her first child in religion, her Co-Foundress in the work to which God had called her—the Reverend Mother Agnes. They were of one heart and one soul. Many words would not express this so cogently as the photograph we are happy enough to be able to publish of the dying Mother lying peacefully in her daughter's embrace. As she wrote in 1922 to Père Lemius: 'I see by what you say that you have understood this fusion of our hearts and minds, absolutely united for the glory of God, the welfare of the souls which have been entrusted to us, and the Reign of the Sacred Heart, whithersoever it may be His Will to send us. We are Mother and daughter, but we are but one heart and one soul. May God be blessed, who has made it so.'

If Mother Agnes, during these last years, had to bear the greater part of the burden, on account of the Mother's state of health, she nevertheless remained the heart and soul of the whole Congregation, and the inspirer of every step forward. She was informed of everything, and nothing was done without consulting her.

We may quote a circular letter which she wrote to her daughters showing the importance which she attached to the practice of charity, and to the union of hearts:

'TYBURN, *October* 5, 1919.

'(Read the Epistle of St Paul for the 17th Sunday after Pentecost.)

'MY DEAREST DAUGHTERS IN CHRIST,

'The Epistle for to-day[1] inspires me to write to you, as to all my daughters in the Congregation, in the spirit in which St Paul speaks. And if I have not the honour of being like him a prisoner in chains for Our Lord's sake, I am nevertheless, by His holy Will, imprisoned in our cell, and thus prevented from visiting any of you. I have thus been meditating on the exhortation of St Paul and have asked this great Saint to help me to find therein counsels and advice specially adapted to the needs of our religious family. We must have but one heart and one soul in the very Heart of Jesus. In the definition of the end

---

[1] Ephesians iv, 1-6. 'Brethren, I a prisoner in the Lord, beseech you that you walk worthy of the vocation in which you are called...

or purport of our Congregation it is laid down that it is *one family*. That is its essential character. We are not simply a group of Houses united together by certain canonical laws; we are *one family*, sprung thus from the Heart of Jesus, and settled in various places for the extension of His Kingdom. The spirit of our Congregation demands then that our love embraces all our Houses, and with a still greater intensity, the Congregation as a unit; that we be always ready to prefer the general good of the Congregation to the particular needs of our own House, for the greater glory of the Heart of Jesus, who has made our religious family *one* in Himself, that relations of special deference and of filial affection link closely each particular House to the Mother-House, and that all our Houses vie with one another in holy emulation, in charity, humility, tact, and tender consideration, in their mutual relations one with the other.'

Then she treats in detail several points with regard to this delicate charity, and concludes thus:

'While meditating on this Epistle of St Paul, so divinely crowned by the sweet commandment of Our Lord, in the Gospel of the same Sunday,[1] my heart felt on fire in the Heart of Jesus, with love for the Congregation and for each of my daughters of the past, the present and the future. I felt that we must be more and more *one* in reality, as we are in the desires and the designs of Our Lord. I felt assured with joy that this union of hearts does exist in a splendid degree, and I thanked the Sacred Heart for it. I thought also how greatly this union of hearts has facilitated in the Congregation, and must ever make more and more real that unity of spirit of which St Paul speaks.

'In the love of our adored Master, and in filial affection towards our dear Congregation, let us remain *One* to maintain it, to cause it to make progress, and thus respond to the love

---

[1] St Matthew xxii, 35-46. The great commandment of the law. 'Thou shalt love the Lord thy God with thy whole heart... and thy neighbour as thyself.'

and to the graces of the Divine Heart. May Mary, our beloved Mother, bless us, guide us, and sustain us in the way of the Lord!

'Your Mother with profound affection in the Heart of Jesus,

'SR. MARY OF ST PETER,
'Superior General.

"That they may be one, as We also are one, I in them and Thou in Me." (St. John xvii, 22-23.)'

If the heart and the mind of the writer remained ever full of life and vigour, the weight of years was beginning to tell. As she wrote to Père Lemius on January 1, 1920: 'I beg the charity of some of your fervent prayers, for I am getting very old (in my eighty-second year) and I have great need to sanctify myself and to think more deeply of that account which I shall have to render to the Sovereign Judge. Happily, He is also the Sacred Heart, and that gives me the most complete confidence.' Always in her letters, it has been remarked, we find this two-fold note of compunction and confidence.

Other trials were yet to come. On November 4, Mother Agnes wrote that the Mother's sight was growing ever weaker and that the oculist pronounced that she was threatened with cataract of both eyes. It would, indeed, be terrible if she could no longer read, nor write, to her daughters. She, naturally, accepted this new trial with her usual abandonment to the divine Will.

This great trial was happily spared her, though the suspense lasted some months. The operation, which could not be risked before each eye was completely blinded, succeeded admirably.

'On Christmas Day (1920),' Mother Agnes writes, 'I asked her, smiling, "Mother, has Our Lord told you anything to-day?" She replied: "Yes, at least I am all but sure it was He," and then she went on to tell me that a little before the Midnight

Mass she was sitting on her bed, in her cowl, waiting till Matins was ended, and preparing herself for the Mass. And with her wonted humility, she said to Jesus: "Master, I have nothing to offer Thee, nothing but my cowardice, my infidelities, my incapacity." And while plunged in these thoughts, she cried out: "Oh! Jesus, how couldest Thou have chosen a creature like me to begin this work?" Jesus replied in this sense (I forget the exact words): "I have chosen thee to show with what instruments I can carry out My works."

'Then He said: "And this work will be a very beautiful one." She cried: "On account of its poverty, Master?" and she was thrilled when Our Lord added, "And of its spiritual riches."'

Mother Agnes adds: 'I think Our Lord willed to make this delightful promise to her, before depriving her of her eyesight.'

The Walk from Tyburn to Newgate this year (1921) was a specially memorable one, as it coincided with the Silver Jubilee of His Eminence Cardinal Bourne. He was good enough to come and visit Tyburn that afternoon, and gave the Benediction of the Blessed Sacrament, first in the chapel, and then from the balcony outside to the thousands of pilgrims kneeling in the Bayswater Road and in the Park behind. He was hailed with enormous enthusiasm by the crowds, and was evidently much moved by all he had seen at Tyburn.

May 22, 1922, was the day chosen for the meeting of the General Chapter of the Congregation, to re-elect the Superiors.

A little before this date, during the night of May 6, Mother Agnes tells us that the Foundress was occupying her thoughts with plans to prevent her re-election as Superior General. Our Lord intervened. 'Calm thyself,' He said to her, 'I will arrange everything for the greater good.' 'Then, Jesus,' she answered gratefully, 'I can go to sleep,' and she fell asleep in great peace of heart.

'Poor darling Mother,' adds Mother Agnes, 'all *was* arranged for the greater good, in very fact, but not as she expected. Her plans had been guessed, and her daughters had also made *their* plans! She was re-elected with unanimity save for her own vote.'

In fact, nothing was changed in the various offices. The only difference from the preceding Chapter was that the Mother seemed to have grown actually younger. And when her daughters advanced to make to her their homage of obedience, they remarked that her maternal kiss had something yet more heavenly, if that were possible.

Up to the very end they had to employ every kind of persuasion and entreaty to prevent her from trying to avoid the inevitable election; and so their beloved Mother seemed then doubly theirs when, at the recreation which followed the Chapter, she appeared again among them after so many years. She even went down into the garden, remarking that it was three years since she had gone there, and as she felt herself so strong, she went all round it; prayed at the little altars which stood among the trees, and examined all the improvements with the greatest interest.

She never forgot the monastic devise – *Ora et labora*. 'Pray and Work.' Mother Agnes notes that even during her last illness she practised it faithfully. One saw her oppressed, exhausted, apparently dying, but the crisis past, she would be found seated at her desk, making envelopes, with an air of delightful happiness. (She could hardly see, and could no longer sew, but she had acquired such a habit of making envelopes that she practised it almost to the very end.)

She told Mother Agnes that when, at the General Chapter, she was representing to Our Lord how incapable she was of fulfilling the charge which had just been laid again on her shoulders, she seemed to hear Him say: 'You will give some counsels, some advice, and you will do very little things.'

She added, with her delightful smile: 'I think that my

fabrication of envelopes forms part of these very little things which Jesus asks of me.' But in return for her fidelity in little things, Our Lord, on the Feast of the Sacred Heart of this same year, gave her an immense consolation. 'At the Communion in the Holy Mass she was praying for all the Sisters of the Congregation at present and to come. It seemed to her that the Heart of Jesus then said to her that He had created this Congregation for His own honour and glory, and that no Sister dying as a member of the Congregation would be lost eternally.'

In but a few months this spouse of Jesus crucified was to begin her long agony of eighteen months, during which would be realised in her those words heard in December, 1870: 'It is in thy heart that I will place My cross.'

Certainly this dear Mother must have been a great friend of our Crucified Lord, for she had to endure a veritable crucifixion. And yet from time to time He gave her comfort as He alone could do.

On November 14, 1922, she again had to receive the last Sacraments. Afterwards she rallied a little, but on Christmas Eve she seemed to be dying. The Sisters gathered around her bed and joined in the Litany for the dying. A Sister writes: 'We went on to the end, and sang the *Suscipe* too. I must acknowledge that all the time I felt against all evidence that "No," we would not lose her, and yet every moment one expected her to breathe her last! When the prayers were over, Mother Agnes, who had recited them, told us to call all the Sisters for a last good-bye, so we went off to tell everyone. They each had a blessing and a few words of encouragement and advice. But I am going too quickly. When the prayers were over, she rallied and gave us, between gasps of breath, unforgettable words of advice. *"L'Abandon, la volonté de Dieu,"* and then she recommended to us *"ma fille aimée,"* and spoke some beautiful words about their constant work together. She promised to be with us always (just like Our Lord). She said: "If each of you is faithful, the Congregation will be always very pleasing to

Our Lord." She thanked us for the prayers, they were what she liked best—the prayers of the Church. And oh! to see her kiss her crucifix, and thank God for all His mercies, renewing her vows. She also asked *"pardon"* for *"tout le mal,"* she had done!

'I can remember the manner and music of her sweet dying voice, the words coming between the gasps, but so distinctly. Mother Agnes made many acts with or for her, of abandonment to the divine Good Pleasure, of confidence and rest in the Sacred Heart of Jesus, and her "Oh, *oui!*" was unforgettable. That is what she has left us as her most precious legacy.

'Now when the Sisters began to come, one after the other; she had a particular message for each. Needless to say, she recognised each one at once, she assured each one of her prayers, she spoke of their families. ... No one was forgotten, I did not hear her sing the *Salve Regina,* but the Sisters said it was wonderful.

'Afterwards, when the good-byes were over, she said never would she have thought she could sing so loudly. "You will sing it again with us," said Mother Agnes, to which she replied that she would ask to sing it with us whenever we did: and she added, "If you hear a plaintive voice, you will know that I am in Purgatory, you will pray for me more."

'Now she began to be full of fun. She said, after making us laugh in many ways: "I think I shall be joyful up to the very last minute." When she had relics of St Benedict and St Thomas of Canterbury and a medal of Our Lady of Lourdes pinned on her breast, she said: "Now I am like a retired general."

'After a while, as a last act of obedience, she asked us to sit down. "I can still last out some hours," she said.'

But she was destined to last some eighteen months longer.

chapter eighteen

A Crucifixion Of Love

THE year 1923 brought a great grief both to the Mother and her daughters, in the death of Abbot Columba Marmion at his Abbey of Maredsous, on January 30. For the last sixteen years he had been a true and devoted Father, whose wise and enlightened help, and generous, warm-hearted kindness never failed.

In March came the Silver Jubilee of the Foundation of the Congregation, March 4, 1898. The solemn celebration of the Jubilee was, however, postponed to the Feast of the Sacred Heart. Father Fletcher preached a very touching discourse, and on the following day brought twenty-five poor children to be entertained, at the invitation of the Mother Foundress. Later on, on November 9, he had the privilege of being admitted to her cell.

In April this year she had begun to suffer as never before. Her daughters were reminded of the vision of the previous year, when she saw herself stretched at the foot of the Cross, and the figure of the Crucified bending over her. And as she contemplated Jesus, she saw with astonishment that, though it was truly Jesus Crucified, yet she could see no Cross. And in reply to her silent question, He said: 'The wood of My Cross will be in thee.' In her humility, she replied: 'Oh, my Master, You have chosen a very rotten wood!'

The terrible sufferings she was to endure were thus made known to her.

On May 14, however, there came some mitigation. On the evening of that day she suddenly saw, standing between her bed and the wall, a venerable figure clad in white. She saw it was a Pope, and at the same time she recognised that it was the holy Pontiff Pius X. He blessed her with paternal affection, and her soul was filled with a profound happiness, a delicious peace. She asked him to obtain for her the grace of assisting next morning at the Holy Sacrifice. From All Saints' day, 1922, she had never been able to go to Mass. And those who knew her ardent devotion to this adorable Sacrifice, well understood that that was the greatest of all her trials.

Mother Agnes writes: 'I shall never forget that day! (May 15, 1923.) It was a Tuesday. When I entered her cell early in the morning to see how she was, she said to me, gently: "My child, I think I have seen Pius X, and he has obtained for me the grace of going to Holy Mass this morning. ..." What was not the stupefaction of the Sisters when our Mother, a little before the time for Mass, came into the choir! They could not believe their eyes. Some of them were anxious, but they all smiled with happiness. She, quite quickly, with eyes cast down, but radiant, went. to the stall which had been left unoccupied for seven months. She heard the whole Mass, and went to Holy Communion with the rest.

'She had again the happiness of assisting at Mass on the following Sunday, on the Feast of Corpus Christi, and on two other days in August. After that she had to endure the privation till the end.

'In September she suffered fresh agonies. On Michaelmas Day she seems to have spent a whole hour in Purgatory. She said that during her long life of eighty-five years she had never suffered the thousandth part of what she endured during that hour. Yet all the time she was praying for her Congregation, for the Holy Father, and for the Catholic Church. Her heart burned with love for the Church! She begged Our Lord that there should ever be in the Congregation, Charity–Peace–Humility. "And it will be so!" she exclaimed. Her death was expected from moment to moment, but she had yet much more to suffer. On November 16,' Mother Agnes writes, 'she suffered more yesterday than I ever could have thought a human creature could possibly endure without dying. This morning she fell into what we all thought was the sleep of death. No one could believe that she could possibly live more than a day or two. She seemed like a living reproduction of Jesus Crucified, as she lay with outstretched arms, suffocating, unable to breathe, but always smiling in union with the divine Will.'

On November 22 the doctor pronounced her to be dying. He said her pulse could not possibly be weaker, and that her lungs were entirely congested. The heart was worn out. 'That morning at six o'clock,' continues Mother Agnes, 'a grace much similar to the transverberation of the heart of St Teresa appeared to be granted to her. Our Lord had Himself told her to expect it; asking her that she would let Him be crucified in her heart. Broken as it were in two, the death-rattle in her throat, her arms stretched out as if crucified, begging for water, she lay, enduring the crucifixion in her heart. With very great difficulty we managed to raise her head so that the Chaplain could give her Holy Communion. It was heart-rending to watch her. When she came to herself she was so sweet, so gentle, thanking Jesus and Mary, and thanking even the four of us, who had borne her up in our arms while her poor agonised body was enduring this crucifixion of love. She wished to embrace us all.

'"For the Holy Father, for the Church, for the Congregation," she cries so often. And then what burning acts of love, what continual invocations of Jesus, Mary, St Joseph, St Benedict, St Gertrude, St Thérèse.

'During her agony she kept crying out: "I am crucified, crucified, but if Jesus wills that I die crucified, I will it too!"

'When the doctor returned next day she was a little better, but her pulse was at 120, and he gave no hope. He thought she would probably die in a state of coma, for already she could scarcely utter a word.

'It was thought advisable to give her once more the Sacraments of the dying, as had been done in the previous year.

This was considered advisable as a new and serious complication in her illness had now arisen.

'The last Sacraments were administered on Tuesday, November 20, at three o'clock in the afternoon. For several days and nights she appeared to be on the point of death, and on the Sunday after Sext, the Community assembled in her cell to sing the *Suscipe* and the *Salve Regina*. She sang with them, at least by the movement of her lips.'

On the first two days of the Triduum, which is celebrated each year from November 29 to December 1, in honour of the Proto-martyrs of the Seminary priests and of the Jesuit Fathers (Saint Cuthbert Mayne and Saint Edmund Campion), special mention was made by the preachers of the great sacrifice to which God seemed to be calling her daughters.

'Dom Bede Camm (I am quoting the Annals) who preached on November 29, said: "Before I begin, I want to recommend to your prayers the Mother General and Foundress of this Congregation, who is dying. Whether God will spare her long we do not know; we could hardly wish it, as her sufferings are so great. I cannot say what she is, nor what those who know her think of her. But we may dare to say that a Saint is dying. God chose her in a very special way for a great work. I do not doubt that the holy English Martyrs, for whom Mother General has done so much, will come and greet her and take her to eternal glory and the joys of Paradise, as the Carthusian Martyrs came to meet Margaret Clement, who had ministered to them when they were in prison." He could scarcely speak, he was so moved.'

'Father Blake, who preached on the next day, the Feast of St Andrew, ended with the words: "I want you to think of one who, at this moment, is very, very ill, and very dear to us—one of the very dearest to Jesus on His Cross. I ask a favour of you to-day, namely to pray that God may spare this life to us for years yet. Lord, if Thou wilt, Thou canst spare her to us yet a little longer to watch over her daughters." '

The present writer, on the first day of the Triduum, received a very precious gift, one that he will cherish as a most sacred relic during the rest of his life. He was seated in the parlour of Tyburn, when the door opened, and Mother Dominica, the Prioress, entered, bearing in her hands a simple, wooden crucifix. She gave it to him, as the last gift from the Mother he loved, she had worn it for years, she had kissed it so often during the long crucifixion and now she sent it to him, as a sign of her gratitude for the little he had been able to do for Tyburn. She could have given him nothing so precious, nothing so consoling.

For, during these months she was herself a living crucifix.

Mother Agnes tells us that during a moment of intense agony, she said to her: 'I am *tempted* to ask God to take me, to put an end to the agony that I endure... pray for me... I cannot ask God to put an end to my sufferings; it would be like suicide!'

'I asked her what she meant. She replied: "God is so good that perhaps He would grant what I ask, out of pity for my sufferings. And that I should be responsible of having, through want of courage, hastened the moment when the agony should be ended. Oh no! I ask nothing, nothing. . . but the holy Will of God." '

On the Feast of the Immaculate Conception (December 8) she was still alive, to the great astonishment of her doctor. With the exception of a delightful smile from time to time, she was almost in a state of coma.

Yet she was to live still another six months. On May 27, 1924, Mother Agnes writes: 'The sufferings of our Mother are terrible. It is as if we were assisting at a scene of torture, or a martyrdom, only it lasts so much longer.

'I said to her: "Mother, it is for the Congregation;" and as she has always her sense of fun, she tried to smile (she can scarcely smile now, her lips are so twisted and swollen by her difficulty in breathing): "Yes!" she said, "the Congregation is a great eater, it has an appetite for suffering!"

'She lies like the Martyrs, on the rack: it is the most terrible spectacle one could ever see. You can watch her poor heart galloping even from beneath its coverings. At night we were afraid sometimes that her cries might be heard outside the Convent walls, and they would think we were murdering someone; for she cannot draw her breath, and her attempts to do so resolve into loud cries.

'Yesterday, during this frightful agony, she kept repeating: "That all the nations of the world become Catholic!" and during the night, it was specially Denmark that she battled for, repeating the name in a tone of lamentation.'

On June 10, she writes: 'I wish you could see the beauty of our Mother's face! She is absorbed in God. She takes nothing to eat or drink. The doctor said: "I cannot imagine how she lives!" He comes every day, but I think it is only that he may watch a saint die, for he can do nothing. He says he hopes he will live long enough to see her Life written.'

On June 17 she was still living on without food or sustenance. She was half conscious, could no longer speak or help herself in any way.

It was this day that was to see the end. She rendered her holy soul to God in perfect peace at eleven-fifteen that night.

Mother Agnes, who had watched by her bed to the very end, and must have endured an agony only second to her Mother's, writes, on the 18th: 'A great peace hangs over the house. She is there, smiling, and as it were, regarding her children. "My children!" was one of the last words we could distinguish on the eve. Yesterday she remained alone with God, and could no longer communicate with us. But I asked her if she could still speak to Jesus, and she looked so happy, and bowed her head in assent. The end came very promptly and very peacefully at eleven-fifteen. Several of us were with her, and I began the Litany for the dying, and after three or four invocations, she bowed her head, and was gone.'

Mother Agnes writes to a Sister the same day: 'She has suddenly cured my foot, and I can now go downstairs without having to depend on only one foot. I am sure she will heap graces upon us. The happiness of her soul in Heaven already shines out on her body. Her face is lightened up by a most lovely smile, expressive, not only of peace, but of joy intense and profound. We all feel so happy. She is so near us. The roses are beginning to drop down already.'

Her last words that could be distinguished were uttered in reply to Mother Agnes: 'Are you happy?' she asked; and the reply came at once: 'Oh, yes, I am so happy with God!... and with my children,' looking round at them all gathered round her bed.

Her habit of thinking of others thus remained with her till the end. And at her death, she spread around her a wonderful atmosphere of peace and joy. Those who loved her best had expected to be overwhelmed with grief at losing her; but on seeing her body they were filled with happiness, for *she* seemed so happy. She was no longer suffering, the martyred Mother, she was the Mother delivered from all pain, in perfect peace with God and with her children.

Everyone felt that she was a Saint. The Ecclesiastical Superiors directed that every possible care must be taken to note down every detail of importance concerning her holy life and death, so that all the documents should be ready in case of a Process of Beatification.

'Her children rose up and called her blessed.'

chapter nineteen

In Pace

THE Requiem Mass took place with great solemnity on Saturday, June 21, in the chapel at Tyburn. His Eminence Cardinal Bourne himself presided at it, and the Mass was sung by Father Philip Fletcher, the founder of the Guild of Our Lady of Ransom, who had proved himself so devoted a friend of Tyburn. The nuns noted that the sacred body of their beloved Mother remained perfectly flexible till the coffin was closed down, and her face seemed ever to grow more beautiful and more radiant. The Mass was splendid. The Cardinal gave the Last Absolution with an unction that struck all who heard him. Many priests were present, and it would be difficult to exaggerate the sense of peace and recollection which inspired the whole ceremony.

During the following day the coffin rested in the Oratory of the Martyrs, beneath the picture of St Benedict and the Benedictine Apostles and Martyrs of England, which has already been described. On the Monday the mortal remains were taken down by road to St Benedict's Priory at Royston. It had been decided that the Mother should rest in the nuns' little cemetery, which had been made in a corner of the park there. Mother Agnes came with two other nuns, and the Tyburn Chaplain, in a car which followed that which contained the sacred body.

Mother Agnes wrote thus of that never-to-be-forgotten day: 'Oh! it was a marvellous ceremony, far more of a triumph than an interment. All was love, peace and joy. This morning we left Tyburn to the chant of the *In Paradisum*. The car which held our Treasure, draped in purple, went first, then our car in which the Chaplain (vested in surplice and stole) was with us. All was brilliant with sunshine, and during those two hours among the woods and country lanes, the view was really marvellous. It looked like a procession of glory following the relics of a Saint. We seemed to feel her sweet presence with us in our carriage. We arrived just five minutes before the hour fixed for the Mass, which began as soon as we entered, and how beautiful it was!'

The present writer had the great privilege of being chosen to sing the Mass, and lay the sacred body in its last resting-place. He can never forget it.

Mother Agnes continues: 'After the *Libera* we followed her with lighted candles, until we reached the little cemetery, all the way the birds sang sweetly, and we passed between roses and every lovely flower, while the Sisters chanted once more the *In Paradisum*.[1]

'Then what a joyful surprise when we reached the little cemetery! It was all adorned with flowers, the cross in its midst was decorated with green branches, the paths strewn with white blossoms, and the resting-place was a bower of verdure and perfumed flowers.

'The clergy surrounded it, and then came the professed Sisters, and nine Novices in their white veils. The ceremony had been perfectly prepared. The coffin was lowered by white bands into the midst of this wide bouquet of verdure and flowers, it seemed to be far more an apotheosis than an interment. All was peace and beauty everywhere. Everyone was so recollected, one felt that a Saint had entered there among her own. Dom Bede was much moved: his voice trembled as he sang the Mass and the Absolution, especially when her name, Maria a Sancto Petro, was sung in the Liturgy.'

And so we laid her to rest, feeling that if her body had

---

[1] 'May the Angels bring thee to Paradise, may the martyrs receive thee at thy coming and lead thee into the holy city Jerusalem. May the choir of Angels welcome thee, and with Lazarus once so poor mayest thou have eternal rest.' (From the Burial Office.)

received so sweet and peaceful an abiding place, what must have
been the triumph of her soul as it flew at last to the embrace of
Jesus whom she loved. We had sung, 'May the Martyrs receive
thee at thy coming!' and surely the Martyrs of Tyburn had
come to meet her on her way!

'Martyr-host so dear to me,
Whensoever I shall be
Summoned to eternity:
Then draw near in close array
I shall need your help that day.
Animam suscipite!'

'Shining stars you've been to guide
My poor barque upon the tide,
Meet me on the other side!
I shall know you everyone,
Through your help the race is run,
Through your prayers the fight is won!'

These lines came forcibly to my mind as we sang the *In
Paradisum*. '*In tuo adventu suscipiant te Martyres.*' Meanwhile,
on earth, as I said elsewhere, 'her daughters stood around and
sang the Church's last words of commendation, and the sacred
burden was laid among the flowers of the garden, as that of her
Lord and Bridegroom had been of old. And now "her daughters
arise and call her blessed," and we trust her Mother the Church
will one day do the same.'

Over the grass there was later on erected a beautiful little
chapel (the gift of the American benefactor mentioned above),
designed by Father Benedict Williamson. And now, close to
her, rests the body of her beloved daughter, her eldest child,
and Co-Foundress of the Congregation, Mother Agnes of the
Sacred Heart.

That dear Mother wrote to me a week or two later,

thanking me for an article I had written in the *Universe* about the Foundress. She wrote: 'You will smile to know that one of its results is an addition to our already numerous occupations, as every day brings in letters asking for "relics" of her, novenas through her intercession, etc... Did I tell you that some days after Mother's death, while arranging some of her papers, I found a Vow of complete immolation of herself to the divine Will, which she had made June 17, 1887. Is it not lovely of Jesus that He caused that oblation to be consummated another June 17?

'One thing struck me very much in that vow. Not only did she promise to immolate herself in union with the divine Victim on every occasion—which she did, and heroically as we can all testify—only asking for herself that God may have pity on her soul, and as she puts it, *"qu'Il se glorifie en moi sans que je le sache"* but she begged of God to accomplish in her in that way of immolation what she could not do herself. This explains those great sufferings which she endured during eighteen months, the very remembrance of which makes me shudder, and especially those last terrible sufferings for the conversion of non-Catholic nations. This crucifixion, in fact, had been announced to her about two years ago, and she had told me of it, but I had not realised how literally that prediction was to be fulfilled. She is already obtaining for us many graces, above all, spiritual. ...

'I think St Benedict and our Mother must have had a very happy meeting in Heaven.'

chapter twenty

Some Tributes To Her Memory

CARDINAL MERCIER wrote to the Prioress of the Belgian House: 'Your dear and venerated Mother General has then left us for Heaven. Certainly I will pray for the repose of her soul, but I will not conceal from you that I am much more disposed to invoke her intercession. I have always considered her as a true Saint. And the sufferings of her long martyrdom will have purified her absolutely, and will have opened to her without delay the entrance "*in gaudium Domini sui.*"

'May our dear Lord keep you, my children, and sustain your courage in your bereavement. You will have in Heaven a protectress for yourselves and for your Congregation.'

Again His Eminence wrote to Mother Agnes, who succeeded as Superior General: 'She was a Saint, in all the strength and meaning of the term, that Mother whom you have had the grief to lose and whom you have the mission to replace. From the height of Heaven, she will watch over you, and be your advocate: you cannot doubt it!'

He spoke of her to the nuns when he visited St Mary's Convent in July, 1920, four years before her death. He said: 'The first time that I saw her I was struck by her extraordinary humility. That woman is altogether lost in God. I saw her again, and received precisely the same impression. She devoted herself to her neighbour with such a marvellous simplicity. You are happy to have such a one for your Foundress.'

Père Lemius, O.M.I., who knew her so intimately both at Montmartre and during the early years in London, is not less emphatic. 'The characteristic of the Mother is that she had reached the highest possible state of union with God. She was absolutely filled with the divinity, absorbed in it, she was one with God. Father Columba Marmion said to me one day: "Mother St Peter is one of the greatest saints that one can ever see. Ever since I began to direct her, I have remained lost in admiration before this eminent work of the Holy Ghost."

'Ever since the announcement of the death of this holy Mother, I have hoped that the cause of her Beatification will be taken up without delay. I pray that by means of striking miracles, she will make Holy Church recognise her glory, her great glory!'

Dom Remy Buzy, O.S.B. (monk of La Pierre qui Vire), knew the Mother intimately, having met her first in 1885. He writes: 'Among the stars, there are some that shine with a special brilliancy. Allow me to speak of your Mother Mary St Peter, so calm, so full of confidence in the uncertainties of a vocation, which she herself would never have deemed possible. Then God spoke to her, she listened, she did not reason with God. God spoke, God led her, God enkindled the fire of her love... Mother St Peter never said to God: "Thy work is too great, and I, I am too little." She put herself in God's hands, and her life became an incessant progress from virtue to virtue, from perfection to perfection. Everything in her was in harmony with the supreme Will of God, Father, Son and Holy Spirit.'

The Abbé Charles Sauvé was himself very near death when the Mother died. At the request of the nuns he wrote a few lines about her. 'Adèle Garnier was ten years older than I. I knew her for the first time when I was fourteen. I saw her very often, hundreds of times, knew her intimately. From the point of view of natural qualities, she was of exquisite character, one in whom one could not find the very smallest defect.

'But it is above all from the point of view of supernatural virtues that one was bound to admire her. I never remember to have seen her fail in the smallest degree, in the theological and moral virtues. Among her virtues, I think that supernatural abandonment to the Will of God, and charity—this last remained hidden to a great extent by her humility—are the most remarkable features of her perfection. The letters she wrote me made these clear, without her willing it. There could be nothing more simple, more true.'

The writer of these lines died March 11, 1925. He was in his seventy-seventh year.

Père Vasseur, O.M.I., who knew the Mother so intimately at Montmartre, wrote, on July 7, 1924, that on the day of her funeral he was in the train, and passing by Lisieux, he saw the little cemetery where the body of the little Saint Therese rested for some years. 'I thought of the cemetery at Royston, and I said to myself: "There also is a sepulchre which will soon be glorious, for the greater extension of the reign of the Sacred Heart." Ah, yes, we must pray for the glorification of the servant of the divine King, who was on earth. the most humble among the most humble. This will be henceforward one of my intentions at Holy Mass.' A letter from the Benedictine nuns of Maredret,[1] contains this passage: 'The earth has lost a Saint, it is true, but Heaven has gained one. ... We will pray with you for the repose of the soul of her whom we venerate, but with you also we will pray to her, and commend ourselves with confidence to her powerful intercession.'

The English Canonesses of Bruges and Hayward's Heath have been for years united with Tyburn in religious affection. The Mother Foundress had stayed with them at Bruges in 1910, and their Superior had visited Tyburn.

I will give a letter from Mother M. Berchmans, formerly Prioress General (June, 1924), to Mother Agnes: 'I need not say I pray for her. For months I have asked a "good night" for her just before leaving the Blessed Sacrament in the evening. Now I ask "eternal rest" for her... but I feel, as all who knew her must feel, that she is rather to be prayed to than for. I shall look on the cross she has held as a precious relic. What a most

---

[1] The Mother passed a few days here in 1913.

blessed privilege for you to have been so intimately united with a Saint! Pray for me to her, please, dear Mother. Surely she will refuse you nothing. I have kept the letters she wrote me, expecting her to be canonised some day. Abbot Columba Marmion had told me something of her and of the apparition of St Benedict to her... I have just come from Choir, and opening our Missal, I fell on words which seemed to me to describe exactly the impression Mère Marie de St Pierre made on me. It is the prayer in the Mass of the Sacred Heart, *Egredimini,* in which we ask to become *conformes imagini bonitatis tuae.*[1] That is just what she had become.'

Dom Pierre Bastien, O.S.B., consultor of the Sacred Congregation of Religious and monk of Maredsous, wrote, on June 22, 1924:

'For long dead to the world and to the earth, she has gone to live with Him whom she loved so dearly, taught others to love, and served with an entire gift of herself. ... Now she rests on the Sacred Heart of Jesus, and that for ever she will be your protectress, and even more than in this life your counsellor. What she has not been able to do in this life for her dear Congregation, she will finish in Heaven, and even better still, for she will see in God His designs for this work, and will obtain His graces and blessings for this little grain of mustard-seed, which she has planted and watered with her tears and sweat.'

In another letter, after speaking of various recent beatifications and canonisations, he adds: 'The good Mother St Peter has left us for Heaven; I have no doubt whatever that one day, and perhaps very soon, her cause will also be introduced at Rome.'

Countless other friends wrote to Tyburn in the same sense, as those whom we have here quoted. All proclaimed their belief that she was a true Saint, and had already entered into her glory.

---

[1] Conformed to the likeness of Thy goodness.

The present writer ventures to hope that the publication of this Life may help to hasten the happy day when she will be raised to the altars of the Church. This biography is, indeed, utterly unworthy of her, but it has been a true labour of love, and he rejoices to think that he is writing these lines on the Feast of All Saints of the Order of St Benedict. And he prays that he may be spared to see her numbered with these Saints on earth, as she has no doubt long been in the glory everlasting of Heaven.

The Vow Made By The Community Of Tyburn For The Conversion Of England

(Renewed Annually)

O JESUS, immortal King of ages, Sovereign Lord of Nations, who envelop them all in the love of your divine Heart.

Humbly prostrate before you, through the power of your charity, taking into our heart England which you have loved so much and which we love, we adore you as her divine Redeemer.

We remember all the graces which you have lavished upon her in making her the Island of Saints and in giving her as a Dowry to your most holy Mother, and we unite our thanksgivings to all those which will be eternally directed to you in heaven by the elect of this country.

Alas the cruel ravisher of souls has tried to tear away from you this nation for ever! How many tabernacles are empty! How many souls have gone astray! Your Heart has been rent asunder. We wish to console you and to labour to repair the offences done to you.

You have always so loved this land! Scarcely had you revealed the treasures of your adorable Heart to Blessed Margaret Mary, than you hastened to communicate these treasures to this priveleged country through the first apostle of your Sacred Heart. Since then you have not ceased to call her freely with an infinite love and a wholly fatherly goodness. O loving Jesus! she is responding to your merciful appeal! Behold, for a century she has been on the way, she is returning to the source of life… she wants to become once more your well-beloved daughter, faithful and devoted! Crowned with power, she will atone for her errors by making known the love of your divine Heart wherever her vast empire extends.

O Lord we wish to hasten that happy day by prayer, adoration and penitence and thus to call down on England all the other graces which you have kept in store for her.

Therefore, as his Eminence the Cardinal Archbishop of Westminster deigns to approve this vow and to confide to us this great mission,

> We, the Religious Adorers of the Sacred Heart, consecrated to this cult, seek to draw down the blessings of God upon the Sovereign Pontiff, holy Church, the whole of society and on souls, through divine praise in union with the Heart of Jesus, through adoration at the feet of the eucharistic throne, through penitence and zeal.

After having vowed the Convent of St Peter of London to these great intentions, we give to it as its proper and quite special purpose, that of representing England without ceasing before the adorable Heart of our Lord Jesus Christ, and in his name;

> We make the vow of offering our adorations and prayer by day and by night in an entirely special manner for England, and particularly for the return to holy Church of the children of this great nation, who are still separated from her.

O Jesus! may the day soon come when all England will sing:

> Praise to the divine Heart
> that wrought our salvation!
> To him be honour and glory for ever.
> Amen!

The Progress Of The Congregation

OUR newly elected Holy Father, Pope Benedict XVI links the Rule of Benedict to the missionary mandate of the Church when, on 25 April 2005 he visited the Basilica of St Paul outside the walls of Rome. He spoke as follows; 'At the beginning of the third millennium the Church feels with renewed vitality that Christ's missionary mandate is more imperative than ever,' said the Pope. Recalling the motto used by St Benedict in his Rule, exhorting his monks 'to put nothing before the love of Christ', the Holy Father emphasised that 'the passion for Christ brought [St Paul] to preach the Gospel not only with words but with life itself, ever more conformed to his Lord. ...' [VIS 050426 (630)]

It has been this same burning love for Christ which compelled the cloistered Benedictine daughters of Mother Marie Adèle Garnier after Vatican II especially, to implant their Benedictine and ecclesial vocation in distant countries in response to the call of holy Church to make present the contemplative life even in missionary lands.

The 'DUC IN ALTUM' of Pope John Paul II at the turn of the millennium and the Great Jubilee Year 2000 found a ready echo in the hearts of the spiritual daughters of Mother Marie Adèle Garnier. As a result of several unforeseen events in which the finger of God was discerned clearly by the General Chapters of the Congregation, it now has eight monasteries in different parts of the world. Each of these monasteries is a vibrant witness within the local Church of the intense Benedictine ecclesial, eucharistic and contemplative life which expresses the essence of the compelling love of Jesus Christ continually inspiring the nuns to reach out in faith and love to the whole human family for the glory of the Holy Trinity.

The Australian monastery was begun shortly before Vatican II as a venture of faith at the request of Cardinal Norman Gilroy, Archbishop of Sydney. One of the first Sisters on this foundation – formerly Miss Elsa Hale, had received the complete restoration of her health after having been bed-ridden for a long time. This divine favour was the result of fervent prayer to Mother Marie Adèle Garnier on the part of Elsa herself and of the whole Congregation. Miss Elsa Hale had been a well known figure in Australia on account of her contribution to the high level of commercial education for young women which she pioneered and promoted in her Hale's Business College in Sydney.

Since its foundation the Australian monastery has received and formed new members largely from Australia and New Zealand. Many of these nuns have been sent on later foundations, and have held responsible positions in the Congregation.

In 1976 the General Chapter of the Congregation responded positively to the request of the Archbishop of Piura, in Peru and opened a new Monastery there in order to provide a centre of Benedictine and Eucharistic spirituality and prayer for priestly vocations. The Piura Archdiocese at that time was without seminarians. However, within a few years after the arrival of the Tyburn Nuns, the seminary was overflowing and a steady stream of young priests continues to be the fruit of this seminary.

Bishop John Magee – formerly secretary to three Popes – invited the Tyburn Nuns to his Diocese of Cloyne, Ireland in the early 1990's. He couched his invitation as his desire to act as a bishop according to the words of Pope Paul VI to him when he was his secretary. Pope Paul had impressed upon him that the spiritual health of a diocese can be judged by two things. The first is that the Bishop engage in a genuine missionary outreach for his priests. Bishop Magee said he had fulfilled this criterion with several priests working on the missions and on supply to dioceses which lacked priests. Now his next endeavour was to introduce cloistered Benedictine life with perpetual adoration of the Blessed Sacrament, in order to fulfil the second papal criterion.

The Largs monastery in Scotland was the culmination of the Congregation's response to the plea from the Bishop of Galloway Bishop Michael McGee to the General Chapter in 1980. He pleaded the necessity of continuing the only remaining monastery of Benedictine nuns in Scotland which at that time was at Dumfries, in the Galloway Diocese, and was in a frail and declining state. The Prioress of the community followed up the Bishop's request with her own pleas. This was the beginning of more than ten years of various attempts by the Tyburn Congregation to give assistance to the Benedictine nuns of the Blessed Sacrament at Dumfries. Bishop Maurice Taylor succeeded Bishop McGee and in 1984 he and two of the nuns attended the Tyburn Congregation's General Chapter and definitively petitioned concrete assistance with a view to final amalgamation with the Tyburn Congregation. The General Chapter decided to respond and once the Holy See had also agreed and drawn up a special Statute to provide for the gradual transition to the Tyburn Congregation, a further eight years of working towards this goal was initiated. Finally the long anticipated Amalgamation took place by the mutual decision of the Dumfries - now at Largs - Conventual Chapter, the Tyburn Congregation General Chapter and the Decree of the Holy See, in 1992. Bishop Taylor presided over the special ceremony which took place in the Largs monastery chapel on the Feast of St Michael, 29 September 1992.

Bishop Patrick Dunn of Auckland, New Zealand together with the priests of the Diocese warmly welcomed the new Tyburn Foundation made there at Bombay in the South Auckland area after the General Chapter of 1996. The unfailing priestly assistance and warm friendship of innumerable people of the locality have enabled this community to be integrated into the life of the diocese. In particular the exceptionally beautiful and peaceful setting of the monastery attracts an unceasing stream of retreatants to the retreat wing of the monastery, while many groups both Catholic and from other Christian denominations frequently use the facilities for day retreats and parish meetings. The monastery church is one of the old Kauri churches built in the pioneering days of New Zealand which had served as the Mercer Church for many long years, and this gives a unique quality and atmosphere to the monastery which is very appealing to New Zealanders.

The 'DUC IN ALTUM' of Pope John Paul II at the end of the Jubilee Year *2000,* was a clarion call which brought invitations from not one but two further Latin American countries inviting the Tyburn Nuns to Ecuador and Colombia. The General Chapter of the Congregation at first felt it should respond to one of these pressing invitations. But as the discussions progressed it became all too clear that it would not be right or possible to say 'YES' to one and not to the other. So a further act of faith brought the General Chapter to decide on making both foundations at great cost to all the already existing communities. This decision had an unsolicited ecclesial confirmation. Shortly afterwards Bishop Taylor who had been involved in Latin American countries over a long time asked the Tyburn Superior General – 'And which one did you decide to respond to – Ecuador or Colombia?' When he was told – 'BOTH', he became silent for a time and then replied softly – 'I am glad. That is of the Holy Spirit. If you had chosen to make only one of these foundations it would have been your own will. But by responding and making both of them it is clear that this is the Will of God. I will pray for you.'

This decision met with an almost miraculous response from the friends and benefactors of the Tyburn Congregation. That is to say – from people of faith and good will all over the world. New monasteries mean building – and building in very difficult conditions. The Tyburn Nuns do not have many financial resources of their own. So it is that the material aspects of these two new foundations in Colombia and Ecuador have been made possible only by the gifts of many wonderful parishes and people. When one of the monasteries placed a notice in the Church porch about these foundations and the logo – 'BE A BRICK AND BUY A BRICK' the response was overwhelming. Even schools collected funds and presented their cheques to help the good work along. By a sort of common consensus people came forward and said 'but so many religious communities are closing down, and here you are making not one, but TWO new foundations! We want to help!'

The stories of the amazing generosity of such good people can be multiplied many times. It reminded the Tyburn Nuns of some of the incidents that took place when the Peruvian foundation was made in 1976. One of the very elderly nuns reproached the Prioress and said it would be impossible to do it because we needed more young nuns. But her most powerful argument was – 'Anyway you can't make a foundation because we don't have any money!' The Prioress replied that we had faith in God. Three months later that foundation became a reality. Even the Abbot Primate of the Benedictine Confederation provided substantial financial assistance because he could see the urgent need for that part of Latin America to have a Benedictine presence which it had lacked since the Spanish conquest and evangelising of the Peruvian peoples. Perhaps more distressing than the elderly nun's expressed opinion was that of a Bishop who confided to the Tyburn community that he was sure no foundation would be made because the young nuns would have to be sent and then all the old ones would die out in England. The contrary happened in fact. All age groups were represented on that foundation, and

God gave the Tyburn Community an influx of good young vocations. So God is not outdone in generosity – he always finds a way!

For the glory of God and the good of the Church universal the Tyburn Nuns remain faithful to their special benedictine life with perpetual Adoration of the Holy Eucharist according to the ecclesial charism of Mother Marie Adèle Garnier, the Foundress of Tyburn Convent, and their hearts throb in unison with the burning words of Pope Benedict XVI and Pope John Paul II, repeated so often especially in this YEAR of the EUCHARIST:

'The Church is not old but young ... and the Eucharist, the heart of the Christian life and source of the evangelizing mission of the Church, (is ever the permanent centre and source of the contemplative ministry of the Tyburn Nuns) ... The Eucharist makes the Risen Christ constantly present, giving himself to us, calling us to share in the banquet of his Body and Blood. From this living communion with him flows every other element in the life of the Church ... the communion of the saints and the dedication to proclaim and witness to the Gospel with a universal ardour of charity towards all ... FEAR NOT! ... FOLLOW CHRIST!'

In conclusion the words of the Foundress are cited:

'We are one family, born as such from the Heart of Jesus, and spread abroad in various places for the extension of HIS KINGDOM.' (Doc. 1919)

The beginning of the Foundress's Cause for sainthood has been started and is arousing enormous interest. So the final words here are those of this prayer that the Church may one day publicly proclaim her great holiness as an example for all Christ's faithful.

Prayer For The Canonisation Of Mother Marie-Adèle Garnier

FATHER, all-powerful and ever-living God,
we give you glory, praise and thanks
for the life and virtue
of your beloved daughter, Marie-Adèle Garnier.
Filled with the riches of your grace
and preferring nothing to the love
of the Heart of Jesus Christ,
she devoted her whole life
to the adoration, praise and glory
of your Name;
she sacrificed herself by prayer and penance
for the unity & holiness of your Church;
she loved her neighbour with a charity
full of humility and compassion.

Above all, she found the SUN of her life
in the Holy Mass,
and so was consumed with zeal
for liturgical worship
and eucharistic adoration,
and abandoned herself with all her heart
to your most Holy Will in all things.

In your mercy Lord, hearken to our prayer:
'Glorify your Servant
Mother Marie-Adèle Garnier,
that your Servant
may glorify YOU'.

We ask you this through our Lord
Jesus Christ, your Son,
who lives and reigns with you
in the unity of the Holy Spirit, One God,
world without end. AMEN.

Imp. David Norris, Vic. Gen. Westminster   27.5.76

If you receive a favour from Marie-Adèle's prayers, kindly inform one of our monasteries listed below.

Mother General, Tyburn Convent.
8 Hyde Park Place, London, England, W2 2LJ.
Tel: (020) 7723 7262   website: www.tyburnconvent.org.uk

Mother Prioress, Benedictine Monastery.
5 Mackerston Place, Largs, Scotland, KA30 8BY.
Tel: (01475) 687320

Mother Prioress, St Benedict's Priory.
The Mount, Cobh, Co. Cork, Ireland.
Tel: (0214) 811354

Mother Prioress, Tyburn Priory,
325 Garfield Road East, Riverstone, NSW, Australia, 2765.
Tel: (02) 9627 5171

Madre Priora, El Monasterio del Sagrado Corazón,
Plaza Juan Pablo II, Sechura, Piura, Peru.
Tel: (073) 377 271

Mother Prioress, Tyburn Monastery.
100 Chamberlain Road, R.D. Bombay 1850, South Auckland, New Zealand.
Tel: (09) 236 0598

Madre Priora, Tyburn Monasterio, Puerta del Cielo,
Apartado 11-01-403, Loja, Ecuador.

Madre Priora, Tyburn Monasterio, Paráclito Divino,
Oficina de Correos, Guatapé, Antioquia, Colombia.
Tel: (04) 8610 412

The Benedictine Abbey of **St Michael at Farnborough** was founded from the French Abbey of Solesmes in 1895. The monks live a traditional life of prayer, work and study in accordance with the ancient Rule of Saint Benedict.

At the heart of their life is the praise of God expressed through the solemn celebration of the sacred liturgy, and supported through their manual work, of which this publication is an example.